Drowning in Lemonade
REFLECTIONS OF AN ARMY WIFE

Drowning in Lemonade
Reflections of an Army Wife

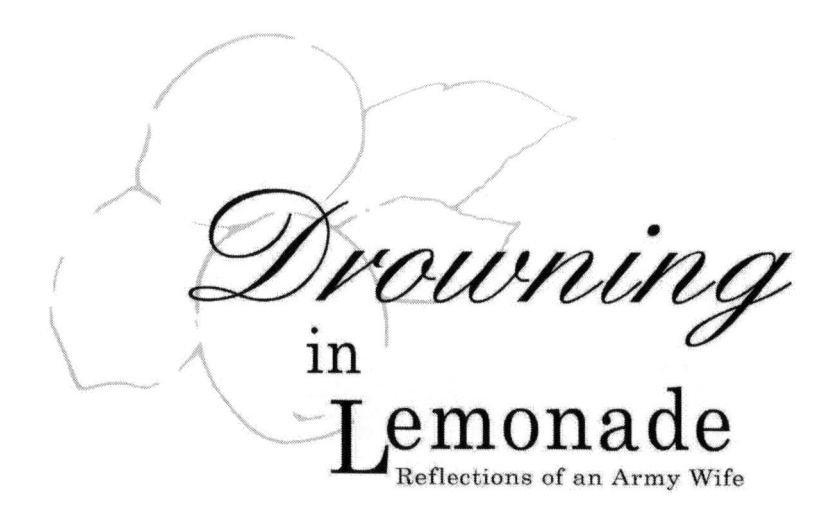

Lynda MacFarland

Mary's Touch, Inc. ❖ Frontline Faith Project ❖ Austin, Texas

Published by Mary's Touch, Inc.

Copyright © 2012 by Lynda MacFarland. All rights reserved. No part of this book may be reproduced (except for inclusion in reviews), disseminated, or utilized in any form or by any means, electronic or mechanical, including photocopying, recording, or in any information storage and retrieval system, or on the Internet/World Wide Web without written permission from the publisher. For permission requests or additional information, please contact the publisher at:

Mary's Touch, Inc.
The FRONTLINE FAITH Project
P.O. Box 341991
Austin, Texas 78734
info@marystouch.org
www.frontlinefaithproject.org

Mary's Touch, Frontline Faith, and the Frontline Faith logo are either trademarks or registered trademarks of Mary's Touch, Inc.

The Scripture quotations contained herein are from The New American Bible, Revised Edition, copyright © 2010, 1991, 1986, 1970 by the Confraternity of Christian Doctrine, Inc., Washington, DC, and are used with permission. All rights reserved.

Cover photo by Patricia D. Richards
Book design by Sheila Setter
Edited by Sheila and Amy Setter

Printed in the United States of America.

ISBN: 978-1974396030

Dedication

To Sean, Maggie, and Philip
my "domestic church"
with all my love and gratitude
forever and ever.

Amen.

Contents

Foreword | The Most Reverend Neal James Buckon, Episcopal Vicar for the Western Half of the United States, Archdiocese for the Military Services, USA ix

Acknowledgements xv

Introduction | MAJ Charles De Rivera, US Army xvii

Chapter 1 | Faithfulness 1

Chapter 2 | Service 23

Chapter 3 | Mercy 39

Chapter 4 | Grace and Gratitude 47

Chapter 5 | Compassion 64

    Rosary for Warriors 72

Chapter 6 | Trust 74

    Traits of Today's Christian Woman 76

Chapter 7 | God and Suffering 90

Chapter 8 | Reminder: We Are the Body 98

Chapter 9 | Prayer Matters 107

Chapter 10 | In His Love 112

    Prayer Service for Our Troops 115

    Psalms for Reflection 123

Chapter 11 | Thoughts & Scripture
Meditations 155

About the Author 164

Resources 166

    If You Need Help 166

Foreword

A VOCATION FOR SERVICE belongs to every Christian. It first led me to joining the Reserve Officer Training Corps (ROTC) and then being commissioned to serve in the United States Army as an officer in the Infantry and Transportation Corps. The continuing discernment of this vocation then led me into the seminary and on to the priesthood. This journey of faith next brought me to serve as an Army Chaplain and then as an Auxiliary Bishop for the Archdiocese for the Military Services, USA.

During my military service, I have indeed been blessed to know countless Service Members and Military Families who love God, their Church, and their Country. Whether we were in the garrison or in the field, in times of peace or in times of war, I have been inspired daily by the strong faith of the members of the military community serving the Country they love both at home and abroad.

    There are many reasons why our hearts may be troubled. The wars in Iraq and Afghanistan have caused our Service Members and their Families to make sacrifices and carry a heavy burden for our Country. For over ten years, Soldiers, Sailors, Airmen, and Marines have deployed into harm's way to combat terrorism, stabilize countries, and usher in a new era of peace and prosperity; and the operation continues. Thousands of mothers and fathers have deployed on multiple occasions to various areas of operations. The Families are affected by lengthy separations and intense anxiety for loved ones "downrange." Some Families experience the agony of a death notification and the subsequent processes with Casualty Affairs. Others must contend with the trauma of a Wounded Warrior returning home with wounds seen and unseen. Children knowing only war for all or most of their lives must constantly adjust to the comings and goings of one or even both parents.

Foreword

In the Gospel of John, Jesus says, "Do not let your hearts be troubled. You have faith in God; have faith also in me."

Faith in God and faith in Jesus is what keeps many a Service Member balanced and many a Family intact. It is the wholehearted trusting in God that strengthens our spirits as individuals, as families, and as a Nation. Faith in God and faith in Jesus prevents us from losing hope in times of uncertainty. Our Wounded Warriors and their Families are grateful to modern medicine; but ultimately, they rely on God for healing, a remedy, or for the grace they need to cope with an affliction.

A wise spiritual director once said that we should accept everything as "gift." God is the source of all that is good, and every good thing comes from God. Jesus gave us the metaphor of the Good Shepherd. The good news is that the Good Shepherd is always with us, especially during the difficulties of life. He walks beside us in all of our troubles and hardships, and He is continually leading us to the fullness of life. Nothing can ever separate us from His love.

He can bring good out of any situation as long as we trust in Him. Faith in Jesus keeps us from being discouraged. Walking with the Good Shepherd keeps us nourished in love and looking toward the future with hope.

Lynda MacFarland's book captures the dynamics of faith, hope, and love in the midst of uncertainty as one military community coped during their Army combat brigade's deployment in support of Operation Iraqi Freedom. Lynda and her family are excellent examples of Christians with vocations of service. They love God, their Church, and their Country; they are a great American Military Family committed to serving our Nation when she needs us the most: during a time of war.

+The Most Reverend Neal James Buckon
Episcopal Vicar for the Western Half
of the United States
Archdiocese for the Military Services, USA

Bishop Neal J. Buckon was recognized in 1975 as a Distinguished Military Graduate and appointed a Regular Army Officer where he served in both the Infantry and Transportation Branches of the United

States Army. Following seven years of active duty, he resigned his commission and entered the seminary. As a seminarian, he served in the United States Army Reserve as a Chaplain Candidate and was subsequently accessioned into the United States Army Chaplain Corps in 1996. He retired from the US Army in December 2010. He was elevated to Bishop for the Archdiocese for the Military Services, USA in February 2011.

Acknowledgements

THERE ARE SO MANY PEOPLE I want to thank not only for their roles in forming the reflections that make up this little book but also for helping me along in my faith journey. I truly could not name them all. And I would hate to leave out anyone who has been a blessing to me throughout my life. So I just have to say a big thank-you to the women and men who are my family and friends, the saints it's been my joy to know and be supported by so often, and all those who continue to be Salt and Light for the world. God bless everyone who has had any impact on my life, my views, and my faith.

I have arranged for proceeds from the sale of this book to go directly to the Frontline Faith® Project, a nonprofit organization that produces quality MP3 players full of spiritual content to support our Troops during deployment, to comfort their families, and to uplift our Wounded Warriors as they meet the challenges of recovery.

To learn more about the Frontline Faith Project, please visit their website at www.frontlinefaithproject.org

Introduction

IN THIS BOOK, Lynda MacFarland includes her battle with depression while stationed in Germany between two of her husband's deployments. She shares so that others might know and understand that the struggles of Military life or life in general sometime require the assistance of others to overcome them. She shares so that no one will ever think she just 'sailed' through her Soldier's multiple deployments without any negative effects. She shares because she cares about you and encourages anyone who is dealing with depression, anxiety, or any challenge that leaves them unable to enjoy the life God wants for them, to seek help.

Negative psychological effects such as depression, anxiety, and other mental health issues can affect spouses of deployed military personnel. Spouses who are separated for long periods demonstrate more negative psychological well-being symptoms than those spouses who are separated for shorter periods, according to the *Journal of Family Life*. There are mental health programs available for those suffering. Military OneSource has a hotline that is available for military families suffering from mental health issues.

Perhaps the most difficult aspect of treatment to overcome is the perceived stigma associated with obtaining mental health services. Some believe that seeking help reflects poorly on their spouses' military records. Lynda's husband was a Colonel in a very key position within the V Corps Headquarters when she sought help. She openly attended her sessions with a psychiatrist on the fourth floor of the Heidelberg hospital where any number of her peers or her husband's subordinates or superiors could have seen her. But her husband, Sean, encouraged her to get the help he knew she needed. Neither of them was ever concerned about how this might affect his career. He is still an active-duty Army officer and has since been promoted. The Military offers programs to help families and spouses cope with depression, and it wants all concerned to overcome this stigma.

We as friends to each other must understand that letting a problem fester and get worse negatively affects progression. If you or someone you know and love needs help, please encourage them to get it. Offer to help get your friend/loved one there; tell them how proud you are of them for taking care of themselves.

The general treatment plan for mental health care frequently requires the individual to undergo a complete psychiatric evaluation by a trained physician who can properly diagnose depression. Once the diagnosis is confirmed, treatment generally consists of antidepressant medications and/or psychotherapy. Mental health professionals conduct psychotherapy sessions aimed at helping patients work through their conflicts and cope with the events generating depressive episodes. Ongoing treatment helps to reduce symptoms of depression, along with support of family and friends.

The idea for a behavioral healthcare provider is to let both the family member and/or the Soldier know they are safe and in good hands if they ask for help. If the behavioral health professional can communicate his or her genuine concern for each member, they will tell their family, friends, leaders, and peers that seeing a medical provider/counselor was the right thing to do and that he or she had their best interests in mind.

God supplies His children with everything that is good all the time. In January 2011, the President of the United States made care and support of military families a top National Security priority. Deployed military service members appreciate that *their* "heroes" are their families. More often than not, the spouse and/or parent in the rear is so concerned and emotionally enmeshed in caring for the deployed loved one that they do not practice health and wellness preventive measures of self-care. A behavioral health professional can help with the preventive coping skills before a situation becomes serious, and that is a good way to be proactive in dealing with one's emotional and psychological health.

MAJ Charles De Rivera, US Army
www.militaryonesource.mil
1.800.342.9647

Charles De Rivera, MSW, is a board-certified social worker who has worked extensively with Soldiers and their families concerning combat stress issues. His research, titled "Early Detection of Combat Stress in Soldiers in Iraq," was published in 2008.

Major De Rivera served as program director for the Fort Bliss Combat and Operational Stress Control Team from 2008–2010. The behavioral healthcare program he established there was recognized by Headquarters, US Medical Command, and the Office of the Surgeon General as one of the best Behavioral Health Prevention programs Army-wide.

Faithfulness

A FRIEND ONCE JOKED that I should be grateful I didn't know in advance what was going to happen to me. If I had known, I might have refused to show up. We *do* have a choice.

And, true, there were unexpected struggles and challenges on my path, but there were blessings and delights, too.

I prefer the thoughts of Christian recording artist, Steven Curtis Chapman, who wrote,

> I may not see in front of me.
> But I can see for miles
> When I look over my shoulder.
>
> Lord, it's clear,
> You've brought me here,
> So faithful every step of the way.

That's been my life experience. Through all the things that I've endured—some public; some, more personal—I knew I was never alone.

I can't tell you everything. There's too much to tell. But I can share some of the mountain-top experiences—those moments that got me to where I am now. Those moments when I knew with absolute clarity I was in the company of angels.

The words that mark "mountain-top moments" are these: "Not my will, but Thine be done." They are said without hesitation, no holding back. *Whatever* God does or whatever He allows, I will accept.

Why?

It's not my call to make. The Creator makes the call.

If I believe in His infinite love and mercy, how can I even think of holding on to any earthly thing?

You want to know how I got here?

How do *you* get to the mountain top?

Chapter 1 | Faithfulness

You have to want to go there.

And sometimes you'll be pushed and shoved.

You'll fall more than once.

And sometimes they'll kick you and whip you.

They'll spit on you and call you names.

But you'll know you're not alone.

You don't fight back, even though you could. (And, boy, would you show them.)

You can't be bitter, although there's plenty of reason. (You're unappreciated, to put it mildly.)

Some even despise you; although you're not sure why.

You asked to know the secret.

But if you'd like to share the mountain top with Me, you need to know what'll happen.

You'll experience some of this. Maybe all of it, in different ways.

I've gone before you. It'll be okay.

How do you get to the mountain top?

By dying—

Dying to yourself—

To your desires, your comfort, your pride.

Look to Me for your strength, to be encouraged.

Unite your sufferings with Mine.

Then you'll find yourself on the mountain top—

And then one day, one glorious, perfect day, you'll go beyond the summit.

You'll hear My Father say, you'll hear your Father say, "Well done, good and faithful servant."

~ L. MacFarland, April 2005

Chapter 1 | Faithfulness

"Moved with compassion." This is a description of Jesus after learning of the death of John the Baptist. He wants to go off to be by Himself, to mourn, to ponder what this means for His life, to talk to His Father. But, instead, He sees the crowd of lost souls yearning for His touch, for His words, and He is "moved with compassion." So much so, in fact, that He stays to heal them, to teach them, and to feed them.

I didn't want to believe that's how we should be, but I have learned—it is. Even as I had the inspiration while reading the passage from Mark's Gospel (6:34–44) about Jesus's wonderful example of compassion, I didn't want to believe it could ever apply to me.

But it does. I've experienced it in a much smaller way, real for me nonetheless. To be so tired, so drained, and then asked to give more to others who do not know what my life is like and don't really consider how difficult it is....

Here's a mountain-top moment: On my knees, I begged God to "make this go away. You can do anything." But my husband's orders didn't change—we were still going to Friedberg, Germany. And so I had to accept it.

It was difficult to trust God's wisdom, to accept His Will. I asked Sean, "Is this the prize?" He had been deferred from brigade command for a year already. The unit he was supposed to command inactivated. The command that was not to be was the reason we'd gone back to an assignment in Europe after only one year in the States. Sean was disappointed and concerned that his chance to command a brigade would not come after all. There are so few brigade commands, and to have been given one was more than a dream come true.

I talked to him about not getting what he'd been waiting for—*expecting*—after his name was on the brigade command list (there's usually about a year-long delay between the announcement listing new brigade commanders and the actual assumption of command). But first, he was told, he'd have to wait until that brigade redeployed from Iraq. That would add months of waiting. I reminded Sean of the Biblical account of Jacob waiting for seven years—working for seven years—to marry Rachel (Genesis 29: 15–30). On his wedding day, he finds he's married Leah instead—*not* his choice—and then he's told, 'work another seven years and you'll get the woman you really want, the one you love'. Jacob is faithful, makes the best of his disappointment; and seven years later, he and Rachel wed. Apparently without bitterness, he just continues to work for his father-in-law, patiently waiting for what he wants, what he was promised.

And, going back to Sean, "waiting faithfully for what he was promised" became a key challenge. Before the list was made public, he had not expected a brigade command, realizing there are too few available and too many worthy senior officers. So, he was realistic about his chances. But once he was on the list, he then had a promise that he would command soldiers in an Armor Brigade. However, a new Army department policy became an unexpected obstacle: commanders at the battalion level and higher would no longer change out while their units were deployed. And so, Sean would not be taking command of the brigade just yet.

While Sean was waiting for the designated brigade to come back to Germany, though, he learned even more discouraging news: the brigade he'd wanted and had been promised was inactivating shortly after its return to Germany. He would now be without a brigade to command, it seemed.

So, we then spent several more weeks wondering what his fate would be. In the end, the Commanding General of Army Forces in Europe asked that Sean be given the Friedberg-based Armor Brigade to command and that the selected incoming commander for that unit would defer for a year. That commander was ultimately given a very fine brigade level unit to command the next year.

The brigade that Sean was given, the Ready First, was preparing to deploy in a few months to Iraq; and, by the way,

Chapter 1 | Faithfulness

Friedberg, Germany, where the brigade headquarters was located, is a lonely little outpost people have never heard of, or if they have, think it closed years ago.

Indeed, it was supposed to have closed years ago. But for reasons too convoluted to go into, it remained open. And the people running the garrison tried. But with little funding for the major upgrades that were required, they just didn't have the ability to change a lot. So, it was a sad, sort of "weathered" post, with lots of room for improvements that would never come.

I didn't want to go, to be part of a unit in which people would die, but now it was a certainty. *"How many deaths?"* was the only unanswered question. And I didn't want to become friends with these women and then have to deal with their grief when their husbands died. I had not spent much time in my life around grieving people; very few people who I'm close to have died. I didn't know how to help, what to say, what to do. I didn't want the pain and the sorrow and the tears. For them or me. I did not want to go. When I said to the Lord, "Make this go away," it was followed by, "Not my will, but Thine be done."

So, there was the mountain-top moment, with more to follow. In the end, the brigade lost 96 soldiers and Marines to hostile actions. The death of each one was so costly. Too many families no longer have their loving son, nephew, grandson, father, husband, or daughter. It was the realization of my worst fears. The news of each death tore at my heart. And I worried for my husband, who felt responsible for each life. And, of course, I worried for his physical safety. In this instance, as in my husband's other deployments, I asked that he be kept safe.

❖

My very first mountain-top moment, in fact, was at the beginning of Sean's first deployment (Operation Desert Shield/ Desert Storm). It was the biggest, most profound leap in my journey of faith thus far. I placed my Soldier firmly in God's hands; and then I said, "Protect him from harm." And I followed that with, "Not my will, but Yours be done." Those words were uttered with sobs and tears, believe me. To entrust my husband's life to God to do with what He willed—it was a realization of utter powerlessness—mine/ours—and a challenge in trusting God's wisdom and perfect plan for us. I never dreamed I would say it again and again.

My husband's spiritual, emotional, and physical well-being concerned me, particularly during his time as brigade commander. He is made of strong stuff, and he has a firm faith in his God and in his Troops. What an incredible combination. And there were so many people praying for his unit, for his brigade, and for him. Sean was blessed time and again with wisdom in the face of difficult situations and with good people around him in those instances. He always believed his brigade's efforts were fruitful in the war on terror. What they did mattered. I could not be prouder of him and the men and women who served with him. And I cannot be more thankful, though it will never be enough, for the prosperity that came as a result of the work of their hands.

"Prosper the work of our hands" is a prayer from one of the Psalms. It is a prayer I prayed often as we began to see the light of hope in the battles and struggles our brigade combat team was experiencing over the months in Al Anbar Province. "Prosper the work of their hands, Lord." Amen.

❖

Another very real concern about the brigade Sean had been assigned dealt with my son Philip's situation. He was going to be a sophomore in high school the coming school year. He had run cross-country in the fall of his freshman year and had plans to do so again. We learned that the new school he would be attending if we moved to Friedberg did not have a cross-country team. There was no one willing to coach it; so there was no team. Philip was extremely disappointed to learn this. So were his dad and I. We also had concerns about what courses would be offered at this much smaller school than the school he'd been attending. Would his education suffer?

And then there was the issue of friends. He had friends in Heidelberg. Now he would have to make new friends just as his father was deploying to Iraq. More big changes.

His dad, my husband, would be leaving us for a long time anyway, so why move? It was only an hour away. Couldn't I stay in Heidelberg where we were comfortable, and things were familiar and easy? Shouldn't I, for my son's sake? I prayed about this question a *lot*. Thankfully, I had the summer to figure things out. I thought about how it was "only" an hour away, and I could drive up for meetings and still be involved but could stay in our quarters in Heidelberg where Philip could walk to school in about two minutes. This would eliminate an hour bus ride to his new school if we were in Friedberg. He could definitely run cross-country again. And he would have his friends that he'd had for the past two years (eighth and ninth grades) for another two years. Everything in my mother's heart told me I should stay. Sean was supportive of whatever I wanted to do. But I wanted God to weigh in on the decision.

Some people may wonder why the decision of living an hour away from the brigade would be so momentous for me. As one whose husband has deployed from within a community of many deployed soldiers and from communities where very few were gone, I know that the former is by far the better situation. To live with other spouses who have soldiers deployed with your Soldier makes a huge difference. You don't feel so alone. And, as the commander's wife, I believed it was important to be there in solidarity with their experiences. Friedberg was not the most well-funded community; we did not have all the amenities of Heidelberg, the headquarters of the US Army in Europe. I couldn't live there and then tell the spouses in Friedberg or Giessen, or our additional housing areas of Butzbach and Bad Nauheim, "I know how you feel" if I wasn't living among them, living their experience too.

A week or so before the change of command, we drove up to see what would be our new quarters. Philip met the daughter of the current brigade commander, a young lady who'd been living in the community and the house for the past two years. She was a year ahead of him in school and informed Philip that the teachers he would have were not that bad (they were actually excellent). We also learned that another teacher was planning to start a cross-country team. They had not had one in at least eight years. The man who was starting the team had already taught at the school for a year but was reluctant to coach a cross-country team until the year we were arriving. We'd been told previously there would be no high school teens in our isolated (from the rest of the brigade's) housing area. Now we learned that two high school boys had moved in just prior to our arrival. One had a younger brother in eighth grade, and the three of them were excellent young people. They soon become Philip's friends.

The change of command took place on June 30, 2005. The kids and I were still living in Heidelberg, but we drove up the night before and stayed in the post hotel. It rained terribly hard overnight; but in the morning, it was cool, clear, and beautiful. Everyone I met was so nice, so welcoming, so happy to meet me. I was overwhelmed. And actually, a little angry that everyone was so friendly. I wanted to hate it there, but I didn't. I couldn't.

That day—June 30—also happens to be Sean's and my wedding anniversary. That year, it was our twenty-first. The next day, a Friday, I went to daily Mass in Heidelberg, as was my custom there. I was a little early, and while sitting in the Blessed Sacrament Chapel, I prayed fervently as ever about what God wanted me to do concerning our living arrangements. I was prompted (I believe by the Holy Spirit) to go up to the lectern and find what the readings had been the day before, the day Sean took command, our anniversary date, when I had missed Mass.

The first reading was from Genesis (22:1–19). The Lord tests Abraham: he must sacrifice his son as God demands. And Abraham, in all faithfulness, obedience, and trust, sets about doing this. But then the angel of the Lord appears and tells Abraham not to harm his only son. God then provides a ram for him to sacrifice, and his faithfulness is rewarded.

I was profoundly moved at the similarities between my situation and Abraham's. God was asking me to trust Him with *my* only son, just as He had challenged Abraham. When Abraham and Isaac approached the mountain top, it seemed their story would end in tragedy, but God did not allow tragedy to happen: Abraham's faith saved Isaac. And I knew taking my son to the new duty station was what I should do. The Lord would protect him. The Lord would provide. I just needed to trust. That was God speaking to me as clearly as if He'd spoken audibly to me in the chapel that day. God's voice could not have been clearer to me in that moment in His presence in that room: "Give me your only son, who is so very dear to your heart, and I (God) will take care of him." It was another way of the Lord telling me, "Don't be afraid." I began to cry and thank Him for the answer, the concrete, tangible answer that I had been seeking from Him. I expected a clear response, and as is often the case, He provided it through His Word.

I then had peace about taking Philip to Friedberg. For all of the reasons I have already enumerated and more, it proved, of course, to be the right decision. I was amazed time and again by things that happened there for him, the positive, fruitful things. And I am grateful; I always will be.

For Philip

When I placed him there
I heard him make contact.

I heard it—
The sound of a little kid
When he takes a running leap
Onto the bed.

That thump when body
Makes contact with mattress.

That's what I heard
When I placed him there—
Into the care of the
Loved One's hand.

And there was that joy
That goes with the leap.

And the sweet
Comfort of it.

Being enveloped.
In the soft
Mattress and mound
Of bed clothes
That you know
From just
Watching that little kid.

Reckless abandon—
Joyful, carefree.

Relishing the moment.
And the comfort and
Security of that experience.

I want to know that
Again.

So, here's another one—

Here's a dream
Here's a friend
Here's my life.

I can lay it down
In Your hand.

And hear that thump.

A lively, playful
Hope-filled
Wild abandon
Kind of noise.

~ L. MacFarland, 2005

As the Iraq deployment for Sean's brigade loomed, I also had grave concerns about how our daughter, Maggie, would be affected by her dad's presence in a war zone and his absence in our lives. She was in the States attending college, her second semester in a new school as she had transferred after her freshman year. Previously she had been in England, where she was relatively close, and we were able to get her home to us in Germany in about an hour from Heathrow to Frankfurt International. Now, her dad would be heading back into the war, where he'd been for most of her high school senior year. She was worried about his safety. And she is my sensitive soul. She can be very tough, but she is vulnerable; particularly when dealing with people she loves.

All I could do is pray for her. And that was (and still is) every day. Probably every hour when she first went away to college, and when she moved to the States without us, and finally when I took her back to Holy Cross after her dad had deployed to Iraq. A very tough time, very emotional for mother and daughter. And "all" I could do is pray for her. And be there to talk or to listen via telephone, or to reply to her e-mails. But the praying never stops.

Prayer for My Child

Lord Jesus,
Hide her in Your heart.
Surround her with Your angels.
Give her only good things.
Continue to bless her so abundantly.
Lord Jesus, fill her with Your Spirit.
Instill in her a sense of humility and gratefulness for her life and many gifts.
Give her wisdom and a knowledge of You

that grows as she matures. Let her understand the friendship You desire, the love You have for her.

Lord Jesus, protect her from all harm—spiritual and physical. Teach her to expect blessings from You every day. Reveal to her that blessings can be as huge as people who love her, as small as a dry, warm bed. Lord Jesus, help her to know forgiveness comes from You. No one loves her more than You. Don't let her forget. Amen.

Service

DURING DEPLOYMENT of the Ready First Combat Team, my biggest concern for the brigade was that the families would feel unappreciated, that no one was looking out for their interests and quality of life. So this became the focus of my mission there: to let the spouses know that we care about them, that the Army cares about their morale and is offering something to benefit them emotionally, physically, spiritually. I wanted the best for our Combat Team's spouses, who were acting as the heads of their families while their soldiers were deployed. The goals were these:

- Encourage others in their distress;

- Distract them with healthy, good diversions;

- Elevate them—their spirits, their moods, their outlook;

- Inspire them with prayer and productive meetings (I didn't ever want to waste anyone's time); and

- Love them.

With advice and input from my husband, brigade leadership, and others, we devised this plan of attack:

- Quarterly brigade-wide events that were fun, inclusive, and not burdensome to those involved, particularly the leadership in the battalions and companies (subordinate units)

- Monthly prayer services for the safety of our Troops and well-being of our families

- Care Team training and implementation across the brigade, with additional psychological/emotional support from our Combat Operational Stress Control (COSC) teams (These were licensed social workers, therapists, counselors, and clinicians in our community who helped family members undergoing the stresses of deployment or following a casualty or other critical event.)

The quarterly events consisted of a Super Bowl slumber party, Combat Spouse Badge (CSB) Challenge, talent contest, and the All-Spouses Holiday Gala. The talent show had to be cancelled due to lack of participating talent. We ended up with only five or six interested people or groups. That didn't seem enough to warrant a brigade-wide gathering. In retrospect, we should have had a karaoke night for the spouses. Everyone *loves* to sing...oh well.

The Combat Spouse Badge Challenge had over two hundred participants. It was a day-long event held on a Saturday, with a barbecue dinner at the end. Free childcare for the younger children was provided through the courtesy of a Boy Scout (my son) working toward his Eagle rank along with eighteen very enthusiastic volunteers whom he had recruited. All the participants received beautiful silver CSB lapel pins, and the various battalion Family Readiness Groups made their own T-shirts with logos and sayings for the day's events. It was not a competition. That's why we called it the CSB Challenge. It was more of an exhibition—a chance for spouses to experience some of the training their soldiers undergo to prepare for a deployment.

The Super Bowl slumber party was held in early February 2006, with around fifty participants, but we looked upon that as a great success. Our soldiers had just recently deployed on the heels of the holidays, and we didn't know if even two people would show up; so, fifty was great! It took place on a Sunday night beginning at 9 p.m. The game didn't begin until midnight (local Germany time), and it ended close to 4 a.m. Only a few families actually spent the night (the "slumber party" part) in the gym, which was in the fitness center on the post. It was a great time!

In December, we had our Ready First All-Spouses Holiday Gala. Attire was informal, and it was held at the Friedberg Stadthalle, where many of our units held their annual formal dinner dances when they were not deployed. We had a traditional color guard (US and German flags only; ordinarily the BDE colors would have been displayed, but they were in Iraq with our soldiers). We also had a punch bowl ceremony, which is traditional, and an Elvis Presley impersonator for our after-dinner entertainment. That was *not* so traditional, but he was a big hit! The real Elvis had been stationed in Friedberg back in the sixties; so it seemed fitting to have him at one of the final brigade events. After that, we danced to recorded music for a couple of hours. At one point, almost every single one of the one-hundred-fifty women there was on the dance floor. It was truly a sight to behold.

These events were all designed as morale builders—and to show that we could gather together, lift each other up, and support one another, no matter the circumstances. We could enjoy life; have a lovely diversion once in a while to take us away from the stress and often sadness of our daily realities while the brigade was deployed to a war zone.

The monthly prayer service occurred without fail; though it was not well attended. But the community chaplains and I had an agreement that, no matter the numbers attending, we would remain faithful to this time. And so, every third Thursday of the month, one of our community chaplains would lead a prayer service in one of our two community chapels. We would pray for the safety of our soldiers and all deployed Troops. And we prayed for ourselves and all of the other waiting families, known and unknown to us. We prayed for the healing of the wounded and for peace in the world. We prayed for the grieving families. And I always prayed for the Troops who had died. Because it was an ecumenical service, I would pray for the dead silently, holding them in my heart.

One time, there was only a chaplain at the service; sometimes it was the chaplain and me. Or the two of us and one or two other family members; a few times there were six or seven people in attendance. A couple of times, I missed due to a conflict in my schedule, like the time Philip broke his collar bone at wrestling practice just before I was supposed to head to the chapel. But in the seventeen months of meeting (we started prior to the Ready First deployment because others were already deployed), I tried to be there with our faithful chaplains. I prayed with strangers, friends, strangers who became friends. And remembering Jesus's words, "...where two or three are gathered together in my name, there I am in the midst of them," we believed our time was well spent.

❖

And in the midst of all these events, there were casualties. Death and injuries occurred throughout the deployment. Two units from our brigade's sister unit were attached downrange to the Ready First Combat Team for about five and a half months. I attended as many of the memorial ceremonies as I could in their community in addition to those in our Friedberg/Giessen communities. For several months, an Armor Battalion from Schweinfurt was part of the Ready First. I attended a few memorial ceremonies down there, as well. We also had battalions from stateside units attached to the brigade in Iraq at various times, and I tried to e-mail those commanders' wives after their units lost a soldier or Marine. I called a few of them on the phone, as well. Those were always difficult messages to communicate, but I believed it was important to connect somehow. Their Troops were fighting and dying alongside ours. It was the right thing to do, and I would pray for them every day. They were all a part of our Brigade Combat Team.

My daily prayers were for the Troops, wounded, deceased, as well as those still fighting; the families of all three groups; my own family; my husband; and for wisdom and peace (the peace that passes all understanding that only our Lord can provide). And I prayed for wisdom and peace for myself, as well. I asked God to *be* my strength because I didn't have any. And He provided. How could He not? He sent us there. He would carry us through. I truly felt the Holy Spirit animate me during the brigade's deployment. I don't know that I could have risen out of bed every morning without the Lord's strength; knowing it was His Will that I be there, right where He wanted me to be.

◆

The mental health support was as important to me as the spiritual and emotional concerns for our families and soldiers. The brigade tried to offer that support before, during, and after the deployment. "Before" included inviting LTC Dave Grossman, US Army (Ret.), director of the Warrior Science Group and noted author, to speak on the effects of war on our soldiers and families. Grossman's presentation to the soldiers dealt in part with the psychological effects that killing another human being has on a person. He also spoke about the effects of constant stress and concern for one's safety and the safety of one's buddies.

Grossman spoke to two different groups of soldiers for four hours each time. That included all of the officers and the noncommissioned officers (the sergeant ranks). Then he came back in the evening to speak to interested spouses.

The information he gave was helpful for spouses to gain insight into how combat affects the soldier and what a spouse can do to help him or her deal with those affects. Statements as simple as, "I'm proud of you," "What you're doing is important," "I'm glad you're a soldier; I'm proud to be a soldier's wife," and similar supportive comments are incredibly helpful in easing the combat stress that those in or coming out of a war zone experience.

The soldiers listened attentively and seemed to absorb some useful tactics that they could take with them and use. Just bringing Grossman in to give the talk went a long way towards showing the soldiers that the Army cared about their welfare. In this case, it was about their mental well-being, which as is now understood, cannot be ignored.

After a fatality occurs in a unit, the deployed soldiers participate, usually at the platoon level, in a type of Critical Incident Stress Debriefing (CISD). We had something similar for the spouses in Germany, too. Our COSC Team members, along with a chaplain, facilitated these sessions. They were for anyone who wanted to attend or participate. Briefly, CISDs allow people to process through a traumatic event that they personally experience. Ideally, the debriefing is provided within a couple of days of the tragedy. The facilitators also provide stress-coping skills and relief techniques, as well as make themselves available to anyone wanting to talk more afterwards.

Our intent initially had been to offer critical incident stress debriefings to the people on the Care Teams and casualty assistance people who were involved with a particular incident after the fact. What these evolved into were group meetings that the entire affected unit's Family Readiness Group (FRG) could attend. Some of these meetings were simply an opportunity to talk and share with a mental health professional presiding. There was always a chaplain present, as well. The overwhelming consensus from those participating was that the time spent processing the event and talking about it with others was extremely helpful.

We were able to assign one COSC Team member to each battalion. Most of them got to know the spouses and were at least familiar to those spouses who regularly participated in the unit's FRG. Some would meet with spouses after a group meeting to continue to process and provide the help they needed. Most units participated in the mental health support plan to some degree, some more than others, but it was available to all.

The Care Team program that I mentioned (we trained close to two hundred spouses) and the COSC Team formation showed we cared. People thanked us for implementing these programs. The response was very positive. Once again, we could illustrate in a concrete way that the Army cared about families.

The Care Team training is something the Army now offers to everyone, but when our unit was preparing for deployment, no one in US Army, Europe was doing the training or had implemented the program.

Chapter 2 | Service

Thanks to a good friend of mine who had received a Care Team Smart Book from a senior spouse whose unit was based stateside, we had a place to start. We researched and found some slides from stateside training that one of the Army posts provided; and with that, and the help of our brigade chaplain, we put together our own slide presentation. The chaplain's slides had mostly to do with grief and coping with it, which we integrated with the Care Team slides. But then we augmented with the COSC Team information and used the Smart Book that the third ACR had produced to adapt the information for our brigade.

Care Teams do what Army families have always done for each other when there is a tragedy in a unit. The Care Team basically formalizes those procedures. Team members receive training, and know their assigned positions and what is expected of them when helping a grieving family. It can be as basic as making sure the family dog gets fed, to organizing dinners, to taking phone messages, or receiving/intercepting visitors. And it can include making notes of things a spouse says, or questions she asks, to help her remember things she'll need to recall later when she's more composed, more herself.

The COSC Teams also conducted debriefings when our soldiers returned from Iraq. This was the Combat-to-Home Transition training. We got about a fifty-fifty positive response to the training from the soldiers. It probably should have been conducted sooner, and there were some procedural problems with some of the meetings; that is, they were supposed to be conducted at the platoon level (about twelve to fifteen soldiers) but one had over eighty soldiers present. Those few were not productive, unfortunately. This transition training allowed them an opportunity to talk about their experiences and get professional advice on how to cope. And also to learn what normal reactions to combat stress are.

Several soldiers self-referred to mental health or medical professionals regarding alcohol-related problems and traumatic brain injuries (TBIs) after their sessions.

This also was very encouraging and demonstrated to the soldiers that someone cares. The Battlemind briefings, which have been implemented Army-wide, have also been very helpful. One of the innovators, Dr. Amy B. Adler, who helped initiate that program, helped us with the Combat-to-Home Transition training format.

My husband and I both believed strongly that if even one person was helped by the Combat-to-Home Transition training, or if one person sought help after their session, it was worth our time and efforts. But we know from feedback from the soldiers that many more than one or two found the training helpful.

I was very outspoken about my belief that spouses should seek help for emotional and psychological issues during the deployment. Generally, my message said it is not normal to send the person you love most in the world into harm's way and then act as if it is normal. It goes against natural self-preservation and protective instincts to say, "Run *toward* the fire,

Honey!" We want to say, "Stay here with me where it's safe."

No matter how strong our patriotic feelings or sense of duty, there's always a part of us that wants to protect those we love. There is nothing wrong with that. In fact, there's something wrong if we don't have those feelings. Seeking professional help to deal with one's emotions is not weak; it's smart. And it actually takes a great deal of internal fortitude to admit you need that help. I tried to be open about this so that other spouses would not be afraid or reluctant to seek help, too.

Lord, the God of my salvation, I call out by day; at night I cry aloud in your presence. Let my prayer come before you; incline your ear to my cry. ~ Psalm 88:2–3

Mercy

I WROTE THE FOLLOWING NOTE to one of my sisters-in-law:

> When I attended memorial ceremonies for our heroes who died in Iraq, and now when I hear of a loss there or in Afghanistan, I often ponder the death of Jesus and the pain His Blessed Mother endured watching His Passion and crucifixion. The ceremonies were profoundly helpful in dealing with questions of "why," especially when I considered the parents or spouses and children of these fallen heroes. Jesus and Mary know personally our pain. No one is exempt from it.
>
> And, of course, I remember the words our Lord uttered, "There is no greater love than this: to lay down one's life for a friend." With His Divine Mercy in mind, I believe our Troops who

have died in service to their country have gone Home. (Note: I use the capitalized version of Home to refer to Heaven.)

❖

At the beginning of one of far too many memorial ceremonies, I told a friend that, as I sit in the same place with so many of the same people to honor yet another young, selfless patriot, I just want to run screaming from the chapel. She readily concurred. And then I told her the two things I was clinging to throughout: (1) this is not our Home; (2) Jesus, I trust in You. The latter I said every day in some form or another. The former I reminded myself of whenever I learned of another soldier's death. It was too much to bear otherwise.

One time, when my daughter was about four years old, she was talking to her daddy about Heaven. And Sean, God bless him, explained to her that there would be no more mysteries in Heaven, that all would be revealed to us—we'd understand why things happened the way they did; we'd know everything. And Maggie responded, "Like how to tell time?"

Yes, her daddy assured her, "You'll even know how to tell time."

What seems so impossible to grasp for small children is simple once you're an adult. What seems so impossible to understand here on earth will make perfect sense when we finally make it Home. That's what I'm counting on. Until then, I trust and remember that the day will come when we get to go to our Father's House, and I understand there are many rooms!

The reason we trust in Jesus when we don't understand is because we do know of His infinite mercy and unending, perfect love for us. The mercy of Jesus allowed Him to die on a Cross for each of us. His love is so perfect and eternal; He would have died if there had been only one of us on earth. Indeed, He loves each of us as if we are the only one in existence, to echo St. Augustine.

I return, as I so often do, to the story in Matthew's Gospel (14:14) where Jesus is moved with compassion; and so He diverts from His intended course to minister, heal, and reveal God's love to the people who seek His help. That's what happens when we pray, particularly in a group at the same time for one purpose, even if we're not physically together. It is very pleasing to God that we all seek Him.

Perseverance is important, too.

"Why does He delay?" (Psalm 13) the psalmist asked. We will often ask why. And maybe we don't find out till we die. But that is enough for me. God's timing is perfect. That's how the saying goes. And I believe it is true.

I cling to my trust in the Lord's Divine Mercy and remind myself that it doesn't end here; it won't end "like this" when things are so very difficult.

One of my favorite sayings (I don't know who said it; it's not mine): "Everything will be okay in the end. If it isn't okay, it isn't the end." Of course, the end of our life here and Eternity in the presence of the Creator of the universe will be much more than

Chapter 3 | Mercy

"okay." The promise right now is enough.

Lord,
I thank You for Your love and mercy,
Your strength and mercy,
Your wisdom and mercy,
Your peace and mercy,
Your forgiveness and mercy,
Your life and mercy....

❖

Note to Friends:

If any of you have heard or read in the news about the "Awakening" in Anbar Province, the man, Sheik Sattar, who started the movement was killed today, September 13, 2007, by al Qaeda terrorists. Many tribes in Anbar Province are now assisting our forces there, having helped push out most of al Qaeda. They are taking care of much of their own security with scores joining the police and local security forces. It is one of the "good news" stories coming out of that war-torn country. Sean's Brigade Combat Team had much to do with those changes.

Sheikh Sattar was an Arab, a Muslim, and Sean's friend. He was also an incredibly courageous man of conviction. He survived several attempts on his life, continuing to work for an end to the violence and elimination of al Qaeda from the region and his country.

Please pray for all of the victims of this war and all those who are trying to do the right thing, good things, for peace and harmony in Iraq.

Please pray especially for the Sheikh, his wife, and their family. He had only one wife, and from what Sean has said, their marriage was based on mutual respect. Obviously, the Sheikh was not a Christian, but ours is a hopeful faith. We believe in a God who is full of Divine Mercy, who understands that while everyone is not blessed with knowledge of His

Son, they can still seek what is good. And we know that all good things come from God.

Here is one more case of Sean telling me about a "great guy" who was killed in this war. It never gets easier; in fact, it is so much more difficult at this point. Calling Maggie at school to tell her news that someone we know has been killed in Iraq, and hearing her say she hopes she won't get any more calls like this when her dad is home and back in the States, especially about someone her father knew, loved, and respected; well, *difficult* doesn't begin to describe it. I still haven't told Philip. I'm going to pick him up from school now.

God can make good come out of *any* situation. We ask, "Why?" of course. But we must not try to explain it away while looking at it with our human eyes and hearts. We must trust that God has a plan, and ultimately, no one can thwart it. Everything is not God's Will; I am not saying that, but He does allow some events to occur that seem more terrible than we should have to imagine.

None of this will matter to us in Eternity.

Not the pain, not the sorrow, not the violence.

I believe it.

Thank you for your prayers.

Grace and Gratitude

ETTAL, BAVARIA is the beautiful location of a Benedictine monastery that has been there for centuries. It was my distinct honor and blessing to visit there about twice a year for the four years of our last Germany tour. I was there to attend and participate in the Military Council of Catholic Women (MCCW) conferences. I think it's as close to Heaven as I've ever been. It's not the location in the German Alps that makes it so. It's the peace I've found for my soul each time I've gone. It was during my last visit that I experienced the "gift of tears" that Katherine Norris talks about in her book, *The Cloister Walk*.

During Sean's last deployment to Iraq, I cried a lot, but never as much as I wanted to or, more importantly, felt I needed to. I certainly did during the healing Mass that I participated in during that autumn night in 2006 in Ettal.

I arrived at the last minute and sat by myself, which was unusual because I knew so many of the women there after living in Europe for several years and attending so many of these conferences. After Communion, the presiding priest began a prayer to the Holy Spirit, which I was very disappointed in initially. He seemed to be talking about issues that had very little or nothing to do with my life experience.

I was taken aback because I usually received so many blessings from our charismatic healing service each year. And I know that God does not disappoint, not when it comes to spiritual gifts that we ask for, and which I was expecting. And I *knew* I was in such need of healing. Yet, toward the end of the priest's prayers, something he said touched me, and I began to cry. It had nothing to do with my current situation, the current deployment; it dealt with something years before. And I didn't just get tears in my eyes; the flood gates opened, and a torrent of tears flowed down my cheeks, and I felt such relief as that dam burst.

A woman I didn't know very well noticed my state and came over to put her arm around me. Then, more women, friends, approached and engulfed me. It was beautiful to know that each of them was praying for me, too.

Then, several priests stood at the front of the chapel to pray individually with the participants. I got up to have Father John, an amazing, inspiring servant of God, place his hands upon me and pray with me and for me.

I can't recall his words; but my tears, which had not stopped and were freely flowing as I sobbed, only intensified during this very intimate, special prayer time. Some women were falling limply to the floor, "slain in the Spirit," it's referred to in the charismatic movement. I don't know what occurs between God and that person who loses all physical strength; but I know, afterwards, they all talk about how profoundly moving and healing that moment was.

I remained standing; but the tears and the prayers, the priests' and the women's, my own, all melded into a profound experience for me, a life-changing experience. I had no doubt that the Lord had touched me and healed...what? My spirit? My psyche? My memories? I don't know which, maybe all three. I saw things in a new light. Moments from my past that I thought I'd dealt with or at least put to rest came to my mind, were revealed to me, and I was freed from the burden they had caused me to carry for close to ten years.

❖

Have you ever done something with the best of intentions only to have your motives misunderstood? Or worse, questioned? It can crush your spirit. For a time, it did mine. But you have to remember who knows your heart, who knows your reasons.

Sean's first deployment from Germany was in the mid-nineties. There were things that had happened then that were still affecting me negatively, even though I rarely thought about that time anymore. I remember now telling one of my sisters that at the time I had felt under attack by evil.

And I think it may have, in some way, remained attached to my innermost self all that time, for ten years. It was wrenched away during that healing Mass, and it was a beautiful thing. Kathleen Norris says in her book that during her time in a Benedictine Monastery, "It was here that I first learned of the baptism of desire, and the gift of tears, the purifying tears that the ancient monks said could lead us to the love of God." I read this almost a year after my "tearful" experience, but I knew just what Ms. Norris meant.

Each time we moved, though, I fought depression and carried the effects from negative experiences that began at the start of and occurred throughout our Army career. A bit more than ten years before the Bosnia deployment, I'd had my first very negative experience with spouses in a military community overseas. I learned then about how terribly destructive a person's words can be. Ten years later, it came to a head during Sean's first deployment from Germany to Bosnia. I learned how to combat the negative comments of others, whether said about someone else or about me. But I also learned the second time around that words not only hurt but that people can truly, deliberately, thoroughly harm with complete understanding and intent to injure; they say and do things that I would never have imagined.

While, thankfully, I learned to combat that experience, I was still affected by it; and my husband was gone for that entire, stressful period, in Bosnia. As if his deployment was not painful enough, my existence on the home front was made more painful by the pervading negative feelings and environment that surrounded me and some of the other women in that unit. And when Sean returned from his deployment, he could not be there for me still. He went off to a new demanding, time-consuming job. Initially, I didn't realize there was anything else to reflect upon. It was over, thankfully, best forgotten. I never dealt with or talked about, nor did I consider, the aftermath of that difficult time in my life. I should have, obviously.

Chapter 4 | Grace and Gratitude

At the healing Mass that day in Ettal, the Holy Spirit helped me to deal with that "stuff" from all those years before. I realized that I had been carrying the effects of those previous years with me, and that had not been a good thing.

The battle with depression I also was experiencing was helped by talking with a professional, some medication for a time, and lots of prayers from loved ones. It would take a long while to restore myself. When Sean headed to Iraq in the summer of 2003, our oldest was starting her senior year of high school. I was devastated at the thought of her leaving the family soon for college. I also was in denial about how difficult this separation from my husband and my concern for his safety was for me.

When Sean returned eight months later—a short time when compared to most, I know, but long enough for me—he returned to the most demanding job he'd ever held in his Army career. He was named the V Corps G-3. As a good Army-wife friend advises, on any Army staff, avoid the "3" jobs. These always tend to be very stressful, among other challenges. To be the Corps G-3 during a war was especially so. Sean never complained; he never brought the stresses of his job home with him. But he was not home very much. And he was always very tired. I made it my mission to make his few conscious hours at home as pleasant as possible.

As I was sinking further into depression, though, that became an enormously difficult task; but I was successful for the most part. At the end of the deep depression, Sean made the comment that despite my emotional state, I was "always nice." He marveled at that fact. I don't. I give all credit to God, who is stronger than anything, and who is merciful beyond measure.

In my darkest days, it was so uncomfortable to talk to people, to be around people, even my own family. All of that is alarming in retrospect, and it was "alarming" to my husband, who used that exact word when I finally told him how I'd been feeling.

Chapter 4 | Grace and Gratitude

I am normally an extrovert who loves socializing; but during that period of my life, I would cringe at the thought of being with people. It took more effort than I had. I actually thought I was successfully pulling it off, despite the horribly oppressive weight on my chest, and in spite of the air that felt heavy as I walked through a room full of people. I literally felt like I was *forcing* my way through a space if it was filled with more than a couple of people. Especially people to whom I was expected to converse.

There was heaviness all around me. The weight of the world was not only on my shoulders—it was on my chest, the top of my head, my arms, legs, neck, and face. I felt as if I were walking completely submerged in about eight feet of water. Sean told me I looked miserable. And I had thought I looked fine to any observers. I understand now why he was alarmed. It was his concern and request that I see a doctor that was the encouragement I needed to make the call.

When the psychiatrist asked me a series of questions designed to determine if I was truly clinically depressed or worse, I answered in the affirmative to all of them but one. A person in a healthy state of mind would have answered "no" to most, if not all. As I recall the one question I did not answer with a "yes" was, "Do you have thoughts of killing yourself?" I indicated "no" on the questionnaire but did tell the doctor that I had been thinking lately my family would be better off without me. I suppose that left me only a short stone's throw away from suicidal thoughts.

Even when I knew I was not alone, that God was with me, I felt little to no comfort through the heavy, ugly oppression that engulfed me. I *knew* God loved me, but I couldn't *do* anything about it.

I met Sister Salwatricze, who lives and works at the Divine Mercy shrine outside of Krakow, Poland, when she was the keynote speaker at our 2005 Fall MCCW Conference. Her words, every time she spoke during that conference, moved me deeply. She is truly blessed by God in her ability to explain Jesus's Divine Mercy to people. Her words reached down into the recesses of the heart. It was an amazing experience.

To illustrate the magnificence of the Holy Spirit, the profound impact He can have on our lives, she described a painting. The painting is of a man holding up a small cup to catch the water that is a huge tidal wave about to fall upon him. I could see right away what she meant. That's God's grace. We get as much as we are open to accept. If we are not holding back, or holding out, or holding too tightly to things that keep us from accepting all the grace God is offering each one of us, amazing things will happen. Exciting things, miraculous things.

The little cup will hold only a tiny portion of what is being offered to us by the Holy Spirit. We shouldn't deny ourselves what the Lord is offering. If we desire it and allow it, we are engulfed; we are completely submerged in God's grace.

"Don't be afraid!" Jesus says it—we should heed His instructions. "Don't be afraid." We should find His words comforting. You don't know what will happen; but with faith and trust, whatever happens, it's not by chance. Faith leads us into the unknown with courage and strength...knowing that God is with us through it all.

> *The Lord is my light and my salvation; whom should I fear? The Lord is my life's refuge; of whom should I be afraid? Wait for the Lord, take courage (and) be stouthearted, wait for the Lord!*
>
> ~ Psalm 27:1, 14

When an extension for our soldiers' year in Iraq was announced in September of 2006, we on the home front were all stunned. The spouses, many of whom had experienced an even longer extension during the unit's last deployment, were saddened, even momentarily demoralized, by the news.

I told a group of those spouses that I knew the news was hard to take, that even one more day was a day too many. I gave them my sympathy and empathy. Which certainly wasn't a stretch because I was experiencing what they were—my husband's tour had also been extended. It was tough to bear. When Sean had called me the day before to share the news, my honest first thought was, "Oh, no, those poor families!" It took about five seconds to process that mine was one of those "poor families." I didn't cry then. I don't know when I cried. I'm sure the tears of frustration over the extension came streaming down my face during that healing Mass. They were intermingled with so many others.

When I spoke to the spouses before a town hall meeting to answer questions they had regarding the extension, I used the following analogy: "There's an old saying that when life hands you lemons, you should make lemonade. I don't know about you, but right about now, I'm *drowning* in lemonade." I put my hand in the air, in a gesture that they should do the same if they felt the same way. A majority of hands went up, and there was applause, as well.

When enduring a tough time in your life, it's easy to deny your pain. It's easier to deny the main cause for the stress you're experiencing or to deny the symptoms that stress is causing. You have to own up to it. You have to say, "This really stinks." Or something like it. You know it in your heart; others recognize it. Just say it. And then you can move forward productively.

❖

Father Jean C. J. d'Elbée, in his book, *I Believe in Love: A Personal Retreat Based on the Teaching of St. Thérèse of Lisieux*, says we should pray, "Jesus, I thank You for everything," or, as St. Paul wrote in Ephesians 5:20, we should be "giving thanks always for all things." If we are to be thankful for the trials and the tragedies as well as the joy, then this is just a restatement of "making lemonade out of lemons."

Chapter 4 | Grace and Gratitude

The "lemons" are those negative experiences; and if we accept them and praise God in spite of them and continue to thank Him for everything, we have just prepared the lemonade. And we are like the person in Sister Salwatricze's painting, about to be swept away into the giant wave of God's mercy and grace. If the small cup is put aside, we allow God's Will to be done—"cover me in Your mercy and grace," "Your Will, which I cannot begin to comprehend, should cover me. I want to *drown* in the things You want to give me. For ultimately, these are only good things, every good thing."

To thank God for everything at all times, regardless of the situation, is to abandon yourself to His Will and trust that His only concern is for you. It's not the physical you, it's the interior you—the soul and spirit—that He loves and wants with Him in eternity.

"My Father, if it is possible, let this cup pass from me yet; not as I will, but as You will." ~ Jesus (Matthew 26:39)

"Jesus, I trust in You." ~ St. Faustina, at Jesus's direction

"Rejoice in the Lord always! Again, I say rejoice!" ~ St. Paul, by God's inspiration

"When life hands you lemons, make lemonade!" ~ Author unknown

And then the negative connotation of "drowning" (in lemonade) becomes an incredibly inviting desire to immerse yourself in the ocean of God's mercy, allowing Him to do what's needed for your benefit. You're overwhelmed by His grace, inundated, engulfed in it; the grace that's there in the suffering is Jesus. Reflect on Jesus's suffering. Remember the hardships and troubles that Jesus had to experience. Unite your suffering, your cross, with His. It will benefit others, too. Because the sweet outcome, the resurrection and defeat of death, is worth it all for Him. Try to thank God in your trials.

"Lord, thank You for everything."

And if you say it sometimes and you don't really mean it, you will.

Chapter 4 | Grace and Gratitude

Compassion

DURING THE TOWN HALL MEETING to discuss the brigade's extension, we also had in attendance all of our community's chaplains and mental health professionals who were actively participating in assisting and supporting our families through our COSC Team. These were amazing individuals: selfless, compassionate, practical, talented, and professional to a person.

I introduced each COSC Team member, along with the unit to which they were assigned. Any spouse could call for an appointment to speak with that Battalion's mental health professional, and they would be available to meet at any time. The community chaplains made the same commitment.

There were several self-referrals after that town hall meeting that I am aware of, spouses who made a call because we had encouraged them to get mental health support. If even one spouse was helped, all the time we spent organizing, training, and fielding our COSC Team was worth every bit of effort. I pray there were many more who found comfort and supportive care.

COSC Team members and chaplains facilitate casualty meetings for affected spouses when families are informed of a loss. The team met monthly to discuss issues, training, and any new developments. Out of those sessions, we began a Bereavement Support Group for our widows who remained in the area for a time. One of our widows requested that we start such a group. It was very helpful to the women who attended, they told me.

Our rear detachment chaplains were amazing. They inspired, supported, joked, preached, counseled, and handled the difficult task of casualty notification. All with sensitivity, grace, compassion, and thoughtfulness. They were strong and stable for family members who were not feeling particularly strong, especially in the wake of a casualty report.

They were asked, not expected, to comfort a chapel full of grieving people at each memorial ceremony in our little community. I went to so many, too many. And each time, almost without fail, the chaplain who spoke said something to help us through the latest loss, to comfort us in our grief. I marvel at how these men, whose faith was usually different from the soldiers they memorialized, were able to so effectively aid us in our confusion and sadness.

A chapel filled with anxiety, sorrow, and questions had to be a daunting audience for these men. And yet, invariably they touched us, comforted us, gave us hope. I have no doubt the Holy Spirit was with us.

◆

To say our unit was blessed doesn't begin to describe what God had given us. The blessings were heaped on, pressed down, and overflowing still. There were so many

Chapter 5 | Compassion

giving, thoughtful, selfless people in our community, within our brigade, and among the spouses. I am grateful to them and to God. If I could name each of them without fear of leaving anyone out, I would, but there are amazingly too many to remember. So many of the Army spouses I have been blessed to know, especially during our brigade's time in Iraq, were the most altruistic, compassionate, hard-working, thoughtful, beautiful women I've ever known. I will always thank God for bringing us together. We were there at one time for one purpose. We gave each other the support and love we needed to get us all through the trials and tragedies, to laugh together, and enjoy each other as well.

❖

We would do anything to help even one individual get through any aspect of this tough situation; but I worried then, and I still do, that some of the spouses of our wounded soldiers may not have received the support they needed. It's the one area of regret I have, I think, regarding the things we could have done to assist during that difficult deployment time. I pray for them every day. I hope they feel the prayers of so many. I pray for what I refer to as the "wounded and waiting" families—that God will provide them with the grace they need to sustain them for the duration of their trials, however long that might be. Whether it's a fifteen-month deployment or the rest of a soldier's life, I pray for that grace; and whether it's to fulfill their duties in their families or to turn to God for strength and peace, the prayer is there every day. As is the prayer for the families who've lost their Soldier, Sailor, Airman, or Marine.

For those who died, I pray always that the Lord takes them to Himself, Home for eternity. The prayers for world peace, our nation, and the victims of war round out my daily prayers. If this sounds familiar, it's because these are basically the same prayers I describe for the Rosary for Warriors (on page 72).

My Catholic faith is an integral part of my prayer life. While I had never been a regular participant in the praying of the

Chapter 5 | Compassion

Rosary, it was always there, always available to me. I never really saw it as an aid to my prayer life; I am far too impatient. But one day, while Sean and I were driving back from a memorial ceremony for four soldiers killed in Iraq—one, a family friend—I was overcome with a desire to do something to help. This was about a year and a half before our own brigade deployed. The Rosary for Warriors began that day out of grief and concern for the families of deceased soldiers. The numbers of deceased and wounded are much higher now, I'm sorry to say.

The following is excerpted from a letter I sent out to my prayer chain and to Catholic family and friends explaining the Rosary for Warriors and asking them to pray.

> This is not the way it is supposed to be. Fathers shouldn't outlive sons; sons shouldn't grow up without fathers. But, the evil that men do to each other is done through free will on their part, not God's Will. Yes, the Lord sometimes allows things to

happen, and we wonder why; but we must grieve and cry with hope, not despair. This world is not our Home. That's what we must cling to.

Our solace is that we believe in a God who brings us Home after our time on this earth. And that our grief as mortals, with our very human hearts, which the Lord knows so well, is God's grief as well. And we get to be angry, and so very sad. The Lord is standing with us in our pain, I just know it.

And let us consider the widows and orphans. We are called to care for them. We are Jesus's hands, feet, arms, voice. Jesus knew sadness and grief when his cousin, John the Baptist, was murdered. He knew loneliness when so many of the people He loved deserted Him as He made His way to Calvary. He knew fear as He hung on that Cross asking, "My God, my God, why have You abandoned me?" We must *all* go to the Lord for comfort and strength. Go to the Lord with our anger and tears. He can handle it. Cling to the hope of eternal life. This may be difficult when our hearts are aching and broken by our losses. But in time, I pray we find healing in His love.

I read in the newspaper that over three thousand members of the US Military have died since the war began in March 2003. The number of wounded in the war has gone over twenty-seven thousand. They need our prayers, as well. There are many amputees, many blinded, and many disfigured by the terrorists' reprehensible use of IEDs. I believe we must do something more—as Catholics, as people in or formerly in the military, as Americans.

These are the reasons why I conceived the Rosary for Warriors. The deployed, the wounded, the deceased, the families of all of them, and our nation need our prayers. Of course, I have been praying every day for our soldiers and their families, and I know you have, too. But it's been revealed to me that we need to rise up with one voice in our prayer and supplication. Rise up with one voice of praise, of thanksgiving for our many blessings, asking forgiveness for our many sins, and earnestly asking for God's healing, protection, and blessings.

Please consider praying the Rosary for Warriors where you live. The day or time your Church or family decides on is not important. Just gathering weekly to do it is sufficient.

May our Blessed Mother unite her prayers with ours as we turn to Her Son seeking His Will; as we wait upon the Lord.

Rosary for Warriors

I believe the Rosary for Warriors was divinely inspired.

This devotion is prayed using the Marian Rosary of 59 beads with meditations on the Sorrowful Mysteries.

On each decade, please pray for the following:

1st Decade: *For deployed Service Members and for their safety*

2nd Decade: *For wounded Service Members and for their healing, both physical and spiritual*

3rd Decade: *For deceased Service Members and for the repose of their souls*

4th Decade: *For all families of deployed, wounded, and deceased Service Members; for the strength and comfort only our Lord can provide*

5th Decade: *For the victims of war, our nation, and for peace in the world*

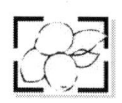

Trust

A FRIEND ONCE TOLD ME, "If what we're doing is the Will of God, the fruits of the Spirit (love, joy, peace, patience, kindness, goodness [mercy], faithfulness, gentleness, self-control) will be present."

As servants, we have been given our marching orders from Jesus. Consider this from the Gospel of Luke (22: 24–27): "Then an argument broke out among them about which of them should be regarded as the greatest. He said to them: 'The kings of the Gentiles lord it over them and those in authority over them are addressed as *Benefactors*, but among you it shall not be so. Rather, let the greatest among you be as the youngest, and the leader as the servant. For who is greater: the one seated at table or the one who serves? Is it not the one seated at table? I am among you as the one who serves.'"

When we serve others humbly, we are servants of the Most High, and we can be Light to nonbelievers. Alleluia!

This poem, which I wrote years ago, has been given to several priests I know as a farewell gift and thank-you for their ministry. I have also had the distinct honor of giving this poem during Mass as part of a graduation gift to the Senior Class at our former parish in Germany.

Can't you feel His pleasure
With each effort that you make?

Don't you know your every move
Immerses you in grace?

You reflect His glory
For He created you.

And anything that you achieve
Is His creation, too.

~ L. MacFarland

A List of Traits of Today's Christian Woman:

- She is forgiving—even though she may not always forget!

- She is loving—even when she wants to run away from home because she swears no one is listening or paying attention anyway!

- She is filled with the joy of the Lord—though that does not mean she's happy all the time! There is a saying: "Joy is not the absence of suffering but the presence of God."

- She is patient—my dictionary says patience "denotes tolerance of someone or something over a period of time without complaint, though not necessarily without annoyance."

And, of course, self-control comes into play with this.

I noticed as I composed my list that these characteristics are all Fruits of the Holy Spirit! These dispositions are not possible all the time—that's because we're human. But we can achieve these qualities in our lives more often and more successfully if we continue to seek our Lord's strength.

When we cannot forgive, we ask God to help us forgive.

When we cannot love, we ask God to help us love.

When we cannot find patience, we seek God's patience and peace.

Now sometimes we seek Him, and we don't feel His presence. And sometimes the joy is missing. But when we find Him again, His presence in our lives feels even *stronger* than before, and our relationship with Him deepens. You can never really appreciate what you have till you spend some time without it. Just ask an Army wife! It's trite, but so true: when real love is present, "absence makes the heart grow fonder."

❖

Women are too hard on themselves. *We're* too hard on ourselves! "I don't do enough (good works); I don't pray enough; I'm a sinner; I'm not perfect!" "Is God as mad at me as I'd be if someone neglected our relationship this much?" The answer, of course, is no! We will always struggle; we will fail from time to time; we'll fall short. But the good news is that God loves us in spite of ourselves, in spite of our best efforts that fail to meet the arbitrary mark we set for ourselves. He loves us unconditionally. We can never do enough to "earn" God's love or get to heaven. And we don't need to!

His love for us is perfect; His mercy is endless. He will *always* love us, no matter what.

All we really need to do is love God. Jesus says it, too, in the New Testament. There are no spiritual handstands required.

Contemplate these words: "Do justice, love mercy, walk humbly with God" (Micah 6:8). What does God require? Just this.

Humility? There is great strength in humility. The paradoxical, ironic Lord of our Lives exemplifies this. Through the life, suffering, and death of His Son, we see how in humbling ourselves we gain the crown of Heaven. Jesus's meekness in the face of the elders, the Roman soldiers, Pontius Pilate...God becoming man is the ultimate paradox of humbling oneself to be exalted.

Jesus "told a parable to those who had been invited, noticing how they were choosing the places of honor at the table," we read in Luke 14:7–11. "When you are invited by someone to a wedding banquet, do not recline at table in the place of honor. A more distinguished guest than you may have been invited by him, and the host who invited both of you may approach you and say, 'Give your place to this man,' and then you would proceed with embarrassment to take the lowest place. Rather, when you are invited, go and take the lowest place so that when the host comes to you he may say, 'My friend, move up to a higher position.' Then you will enjoy the esteem of your companions at the table. For everyone who exalts himself will be humbled, but the one who humbles himself will be exalted."

And, of course, the victory of Jesus's death on the Cross is the paradox of the death part. In 1 Corinthians 1:18–19, 25, Paul writes, "The message of the Cross is foolishness to those who are perishing, but to us who are being saved it is the power of God. For it is written: 'I will destroy the wisdom of the wise, and the learning of the learned I will set aside'...For the foolishness of God is wiser than human wisdom, and the weakness of God is stronger than human strength."

That's where the Victory is achieved: Jesus's life, His words, His Passion and death are so contrary to the way the world says we ought to live. But He's our shining example. Back to that strength in humility idea, right? As believers, we don't see our successes or failures, our weaknesses or strengths through men's eyes, but through Heaven's!

The unvarnished truth is we are imperfect instruments. As a Type A personality in so many ways, this is something I didn't care to admit or contemplate. How can I share my faith, love of God, and trust in His mercy when I am *so flawed?*

I tell you not to worry; then I worry. I tell you to forget your past sins—they are forgiven; but still I feel guilt over sins I know God has long ago forgiven me.

I tell you not to doubt, but then I feel all alone and anxious; doubt creeps in....

It's not about me, though. Thank God! In fact, I have to become smaller and smaller and let Jesus shine through. I have to become so humble that I disappear. And then people see Jesus when they look at me. And when I see with Jesus's eyes, I see everyone with love and mercy; it becomes so easy to love them.

My prayer is this: Let me see Jesus in others. And let them see Jesus in me, especially the ones who weren't looking for Him! What a sweet surprise. And I'm the one who gets to "spring" it! But all the glory is His.

In dying to myself, I receive great power and strength. It's one of those blessed paradoxes. "When I am weak, I am made strong," and I find the words of St. Paul are Truth!

In the Gospel of John 3:30, we read, "He must increase; I must decrease" from John the Baptist, who is speaking about Jesus and His ministry. What humility. John was beloved and revered by his followers and feared by some very influential people in the community. He had "stature," but he willingly, selflessly gave it up for the good of everyone—for God's plan. His followers didn't understand. But he did; and he knew the obligation that wisdom and knowledge burden us with: to do the right thing even when everyone else questions or thinks we're stupid or crazy.

What John did, that's what we are asked to do, too. When you open yourself to God's plan, you find such peace and joy. And you receive the grace that pours upon you like that tidal wave in Sister Salwatricze's painting.

Then there's the strength of the Lord to see you through the challenges of life. "The joy of the Lord is my strength." "I can do all things through Christ who strengthens me." Sound familiar? It's all there, the promises of God, to get you through. To get me through.

When you are asked to serve but don't get mentioned, work and are ignored, or help and get no thanks, it can be quite discouraging. But once I came to realize, to acknowledge, that God was working through me, I wasn't nervous or upset anymore. I wasn't resentful or hurt. I was actually joyful! I wasn't afraid of failure (if I happened to be in charge). Actually, failure never entered my thoughts as a possible outcome when I tried something new. Praise God! He was taking care of everything. Part of that grace is wisdom from the Holy Spirit. Wisdom is knowing what to do, knowing what to say, knowing what's right, and also accepting the "not now, child" moments.

In asking the Lord to be my strength, I grew in my faith. I remember a time in my life when I kept asking the Lord to use me. It took months before I realized that He had been all along! I was feeding the hungry, visiting the sick; I was teaching the faith through faith formation classes. It was happening in spite of my blindness. Crucial elements: trusting He would answer me, working to advance the Kingdom, using the model of Jesus, that is, compassion for the needs of others...we can *all* do this.

God will use anyone to complete His plan, even unwilling or unsuspecting people, but how much more is accomplished when we work willingly with Him? We don't have to say, "I'm not smart enough" or "I'm not good enough." God wants willing hearts. That's all. It won't be you doing those dramatic, amazing things or little things that are amazing. It will be God working through you, if you'll only invite Him.

And are there still moments of weakness, moments of hesitation, moments of guilt over sin long since forgiven and forgotten? Yes. But I'm human, and God understands. He knows our hearts. The intentions are blessed. Perhaps, as I continue on my journey (and we're all on a journey), I'll get past those occasional but all too real negative feelings. Doubt, guilt, worry—these are obviously not of God.

Just keep praying your way through them. I prayed even when I felt nothing. I just *knew* God was listening and was anguishing with me. I just *knew* God heard my cries, my spirit groaning. I *knew* He had not abandoned me. Even when it didn't feel that way.

Open yourself up to grace. Don't resist. Don't be afraid.

There's a song, "Strollin' on the Water" by Bryan Duncan, that deals with this experience. When Peter gets out of the boat to walk toward Jesus, he doubts—and he sinks. In the song, we imagine ourselves "strolling" on the water. We don't hurry toward Jesus to ensure we won't go under. We don't worry about the waves and wind knocking us down. Strolling connotes a carefree, casual walk toward our destination. Our sojourn on the water with Jesus should be worry-free. Remember, Jesus says on a few occasions in Scripture, "Don't be afraid." He says it to the apostles; He is saying it to us.

Strollin' on the water—that's what our faith should be in hard times—or any time.

◆

Matthew 14:22-33

He reached out His arm,
Put out His hand.
He wasn't angry; He wasn't worried.
He was serene, peaceful.
Even as the waves whipped around us,
Even as the wind tore past us,
Through our clothes,
He was strong.

I wavered.
He never did.
I hesitated.
He only moved that much quicker
To save me.

I cried out for help.
And He was moved with compassion.

Again. For me.
For everyone.
He is always looking on us in love.
He is not condemning us for our fear,
Our hesitancy,

Chapter 6 | Trust

Our lack of faith.

He is only loving us and asking us
To trust Him and His mercy.

I was so sorry I let Him down.
He forgave me.
Again.
Me. Everyone.

He is so ready to forgive us in His love.
Washing away our sins so
It's like we never sinned.
Even as the world pushes in around us;
Even as we are torn by life's choices.

He is strong. Let Him be your strength.
He always can be.
If we just ask.
He's waiting to be asked.

Don't hesitate.
He'll move in so quickly to save you.
Cry out for help.
And He will be moved with compassion.

When you get out of the boat and you start to sink, He'll reach out His arm for you to take His hand.

~ L. MacFarland

As one who was always so fearful when I was younger, Jesus's words had (and still have) great impact upon me. I learned not to be afraid of so many things when I followed His direction not to worry.

And when I remind myself of His "don't be afraid" admonishment, I truly stop fearing. Whether it's the unknown, the imagined, or the very real, I've learned to stop fearing. And then we are back to our "Trust in Him." To be unafraid because Jesus says so, that's trust.

If only I could constantly remember. But, as I go along my journey, I'm getting better!

"Jesus, I trust in You." Go ahead, say it. Out loud! And really mean it. Give your fears over to Him. Give your troubles to Him. When I prayed for the deployed soldiers in the brigade, I would imagine tiny little figures tumbling gently into an enormous hand. I was, in my mind's eye, placing them all in God's hands for His care. His very capable hands—His *perfectly*

capable hands—as I have said for years—
the safest place to be.

God and Suffering

THERE ARE THREE THINGS I know:

- We aren't Home yet.
- I trust in Jesus's merciful love.
- I don't belong to any mortal; no one belongs to me.

Do I live stress free? No. Am I perfectly accepting of all occurrences? No. Am I able to give up what "control" I think I have? Not usually, not without a fight.

I'm an imperfect human being. So are you. And God loves us anyway. I think He loves us even more when we stumble or fall.

Imagine a toddler just learning to walk. As a parent, you can watch that little kid wobble and fall, and you just love them so much more in that instant. And of what is that instant composed? Sympathy, empathy, joy, compassion.

Chapter 7 | God and Suffering

Sympathy: "I'm sorry you fell."

Empathy: "I know what it's like to fall."

Joy: "You are adorable."

Compassion: "Let me help you up now."

God says all of those things to us when we falter, or fail to live up to our potential, or when we sin. While He who is all good has not sinned, He took our sins upon Himself on the Cross. He knows what sin is and how it hurts.

Of course, it is most difficult to say "I trust in You" in times of sorrow and suffering—when tragedy strikes and things don't make sense: the death of a child, the untimely death of anyone (which particularly resonates in this time of war with so many dying), people suffering with chronic illnesses or fatal diseases, poverty, tsunamis, famine, earthquakes—the devastation of any natural disaster. How do we come to grips with all that? How do we reconcile the love of God with life's pain?

I wrote the following late one night in response to an e-mail from a friend who was struggling with the question "Where is God?" in a world so full of violence, hatred, and suffering. I had been spending time with Sister Salwatricze, and I am certain that her prayers were heard as I had told her about my friend's questions and my uncertainty in answering them. God is good. He heard her prayers on my behalf. Here is my reply:

> All I can tell you is that I believe this is not our Home, that where we're headed will be infinitely better than anything we could imagine as perfection.
>
> Here we are physical/spiritual beings. In the age to come we cannot imagine how complete our joy will be in the presence of the Creator...when we will be "like angels" (Luke 20:36). I believe God is all powerful and that He is as involved in our lives as we allow Him to be. I believe that He can make good come out of any situation, no matter how terrible.

Chapter 7 | God and Suffering

I believe that we are called to be His hands, feet, voice, eyes, and ears many times. I believe in His mercy. Every tear will not only be wiped away, but the suffering, no matter how severe, will not even be a distant memory in eternity with the Lord.

I have known people who have suffered deeply and experienced great loss, and they still love and trust God. His ways are so much greater than ours. We will never understand it all on this earthly plane. So, I pray, and I say, "Thy Will be done." And then I pray some more.

I *trust* in His mercy, His infinite love for each one of us. He cannot give us anything that is evil. He is all good. We bring evil upon ourselves. Where is God? He is right here beside us, within us. He is being beaten while tied to a pillar. He is lying in anguish, face down in the dirt asking not to die, He is experiencing razor sharp thorns piercing His scalp and nails piercing His hands and feet. He is feeling the spear in His side. He is gasping for breath as He hangs on the Cross. He is cursed and spit on and is yelled at, lied about—and yet makes no reply.

If I believe Jesus is God, He did not deserve even one moment of His Passion. If He is our Savior, He could not avoid it. He is the supreme example of something Very Good coming out of something seemingly evil. All He desires is to love us, forgive us, to bring us to Himself. I don't know what Heaven will be like; I just know that He promised that He'll be there when we arrive.

Much more could be discussed. These are things I believe. They are not up for debate. Just a way of explaining why I refuse to despair or be forever angry about things that happen in the world, in my life....(Excerpt from an e-mail written in 2007 to a friend's daughter who was at that time a student at Virginia Tech. This followed in response to the shootings that occurred there in April of that year, and it was shortly after my husband and his brigade had returned from Iraq.)

❖

I cling to certain things during times of adversity, and one of them is this: "Do not fix your eyes on the affliction surrounding you. Turn your eyes upon the risen Lord, who has all power in Heaven and on earth. His help will come" (M. Basilea Schlink).

I have seen very good things come out of evil. I have seen the best in human beings revealed even during the most terrible times. I have been inspired by the goodness of human nature and awed by the selflessness of others. Where is God when horrible events occur? He is within each one of us who still strives to do what is right; He is weeping with us in our pain. He consoles us through the hands, and feet, and voices of others. We can lift up our loved ones and those who suffer to Him and ask for His healing presence and comfort and love.

I continue to trust in God and remind myself that this world is not our Home.

Jesus said, "Blessed are you who mourn; you shall be comforted." That is one prayer I have uttered repeatedly over the past year or so: "Lord, comfort those who mourn." He knows what they need; I just leave it at that.

The other thing Jesus told us to do is ask our Father to "Deliver us from evil." This I have also often repeated in recent months. I don't know if this helps anyone, but it helps me, and I felt moved to share it.

I talk to God frequently and believe He does not desert us; I often feel His presence; I see His works in action. Of course, I question and ask why. Of course, I get angry. Of course, I cry.

Matt LePorte and Dr. Liviu Librescu, the student and professor who gave their lives during the shooting at Virginia Tech so that others might live, are two of the people whose stories have brought me to tears. We have got to be positive agents and work for the good of our brothers and sisters. We have got to share our compassion with all who suffer.

We outnumber those who do evil; they are just capable of doing profound damage. But I pray that we continue to do the best we can, be the best we can, think outside ourselves as much as we can, so that the good things we do enlarge God's love in our world. He expects no less from us as Christians.

Reminder:

We Are the Body

I WROTE THE FOLLOWING LETTER to the editor of the *Stars and Stripes* newspaper, European edition; and it appeared on Sunday, January 16, 2005. An editorial had been published on January 5 by columnist Tom Schaefer questioning the existence of God in the aftermath of the tsunami in Indonesia around Christmas in 2004. He saw it as a "challenge for the faithful." This was my response:

> For the Christian, the ultimate comfort is knowing this world is not our Home. We face earthly experiences armed with eternal realities. While we cannot explain such devastation caused by the tsunami in those countries, we know that God was and is with those

affected by this catastrophe. The hands, feet, and voice of our Lord will be known through the actions of rescuers from so many different places and even from survivors who think of, or thought of, others before themselves.

We can be His hands, as well.

Our strength as witnesses of the destruction's aftermath is in knowing we are not helpless; we can pray for our brothers and sisters who suffer. We ask God's angels to minister to the wounded, no matter how, until medical or spiritual aid arrives. And when we are "moved with compassion," as Jesus is so often described in the New Testament, we fall to our knees in prayer for others' well-being, and those prayers have great effect. And, of course, so many will donate money and supplies out of their willing spirits' desire to help.

I do not question whether God exists, or whether He is all good. I know both to be true. I also know that we are not Home yet, and we need to always look up and out, instead of within, if we are to find the Creator of the universe. Trusting in Him makes all the difference when tragedies arise, either in our own lives or when we see them in the lives of others.

He Is Lord to All

Don't let fear control you.
Don't let sorrow consume you.
Don't let worry cover you.
Don't give evil more credit than it deserves!
We can overcome evil with Good!
God is good;
God is love;
God is omnipotent—
We know He has the victory.

~ L. MacFarland

My daughter once asked me if I really believe God has a plan for each of us. I told her that I believe God has a plan for the salvation of the world; and yet, I also believe He is as involved in our lives as we allow Him.

When our family was stationed in Vilseck, Germany, my daughter and I had the pleasure of being members of the Bavarian Arts Guild (BAG), a community theater group. It was a great experience; and Maggie and I both sang, danced, and acted on stage many times for the people of our community. It was always fun and rewarding.

Before our family moved back to the States, the BAG leadership considered several shows for their spring production; *Godspell* was listed among them. The musical is based on the Gospel of Matthew, and it is entertaining as well as educational and very inspiring for many. I was so excited because I had loved that show since I was in college and thought it was a perfect opportunity to share God's Word without being heavy handed or "churchy." Now, none of the people in charge of deciding which show would be produced was terribly on fire in their faith; in fact, one of the two decision makers, Terry, was an agnostic. She wasn't even sure if she believed in God. She often told me she "envied my faith," as I was very open about it. Terry and Frank, who would be the director, were still considering other shows when I told them I just knew God wanted us to do *Godspell*.

"God doesn't care what show the Bavarian Arts Guild does," came the reply. And that's when I said, "I am going to tell you the same thing I tell my children: God will be as involved in our lives as we allow Him." Why would He not want us to perform this wonderful, inspiring show? Everything was in place for this to be accomplished.

Terry said, as a way of throwing up an obstacle, "Well, we'd need a rock band."

"I have one!" was my reply. My husband's battalion had a rock band that had just come in second in a battle of the bands competition (in which 'everyone' said they should have won!). I asked the lead

Chapter 8 | Reminder: We Are the Body

guitarist if they were interested. Of course they were!

Then the leadership was concerned we didn't have enough strong singers. I talked our Catholic choir leader (who "never had time") into doing the show. She was marvelous!

One of the company commanders from another unit was told by his battalion commander that he could have time off to come to rehearsal while his unit was at gunnery training. Unheard of! He was our John/Judas. He was amazing!

No one else in the show had training or field time during rehearsals or the performances. That 'never' happens! We had more soldiers in this show than any before.

Next, the dates ended up being during Lent, and our last performance was actually on Palm Sunday. Couldn't have been more perfect! What a blessing.

And then, during rehearsals, there were questions from cast members and stage hands about the Gospel. What an opportunity!

During and after the performances, many were touched by the show. Audience members and cast alike would often be in tears by the end. Every night before the performance, our John/Judas would lead us together, cast and crew, backstage in prayer. He was Southern Baptist and would give such inspiring prayers before we went on. He would pray that we would bless the audience and bring people to Jesus. No one ever objected to his prayers—not the Jewish music director, who joined us; not the agnostic; not the nonpracticing Catholic; nor anyone else. It was an amazing experience. And all of this was accomplished with God's timing and His involvement in our little theater company.

A year and a half later, we returned to Germany, and I got a phone call from Terry. She wanted to let me know that she'd become a Christian since we'd left Vilseck. And she said that I had been one of a few bright lights on a very dark road. Praise God! I would not have had the joy of knowing Terry's conversion of heart had I not been willing to let God use me, to risk ridicule for my beliefs. It never occurred to me that I should be worried about it. I was doing what God wanted me to do. Our faith is an active faith! We have a part to play in God's plan.

Here are some things we can do (inspired by an article from *The Word Among Us* magazine):

- *Don't just stand there!* Lip service disappoints everyone and satisfies no one—especially God.

- *Read Scripture—and other edifying books.* Father David Knight says that to read the Bible is "to know the mind of God." Who wouldn't want that?

- *Talk about what God is revealing to you.* Your insights when discussing them with others will edify them, and their sharing will often lead you to new insights! Talk to God. Prayer is conversation with God. Expect an answer!

- *Listen to Jesus.* He is calling us out of the boat. He is telling us to keep our eyes on Him. Hear to His words, "Don't be afraid." It's the same as "Jesus, I trust in You." Climbing out of the boat, onto the rough seas, and walking toward our Lord is "Thy Will be done" in action.

Father God, Creator of the Universe:
Be our strength, for we have none.
With Yours, we can do anything.

Jesus Christ, True God and True Man,
Have mercy on us;
We trust in You.

Holy Spirit of the Living God,
Give us wisdom
To understand Your Will for us,
Courage to defend our faith,
And words to share the Good News.

Grant us patience with those who don't know You. And for our weary and troubled souls, grant us peace. Amen!

Prayer Matters

ONE IDEA I'd like you to take away from this book if you remember nothing else: You can pray anywhere, anytime!

Marilyn Norquist Gustin writes, "Today I am inclined to talk to God any time, any place and even without reason. As thinking 'to God' instead of 'about God' became habitual, prayer began to seep into all of life instead of being reserved for particular times and places. Now, conversation with God is a living experience."

This is my experience, too. I just talk to God all the time. I'm uncertain where my thoughts end and my prayers begin. And if we dedicate our days to God when we rise in the morning, every action, frustration, bit of suffering, and joy is like a living prayer.

I could spend all my days
Praising You—
In song, with words.

But what about their homework?
And the game?

I could spend all my days
Praising You—
On my knees, hands raised.

But instead, I'm on my knees
Scrubbing a stain out of the rug.

I could spend all my days
Praising You—
In fellowship with other believers.

But then I'd miss
The "fascinating" monologue
From the old woman in the bank line
Who tells me about her children
Who never call.

I could spend all my days
Praising You—
And I do.

You are there in the lullaby
I sing to the drowsy child.
You are there when I'm on my knees

Picking up the little one
With upraised arms.

You are there wherever there's
A lonely soul, just as surely
As You're there in the overflowing
Church at Christmas.

I can praise You with my life
If I remember You are there—

And I call upon Your Name
And wisdom
And strength
In thanksgiving and in awe...
That You are always there.

~ L. MacFarland

We need to be aware of God's responses when we pray. Yes, prayer is talking to God, but it's also listening. And He does reply. Sometimes, we miss that part.

God is speaking to us. Are you listening? Are you asking Him questions and then waiting for an answer? Are you ready to accept that He's there, that He loves you, even when the answer is "no"? Or when He's slow in His response? Expect an answer. It is out there. It can come in so many ways. We are so impatient. And sometimes we can't hear the answer because we're distracted by the noise or worries of our lives. God's actually always talking to each of us. We need to learn to listen, to see. The closer we grow in our relationship with Him, the better we'll be at hearing Him, at seeing Him, at understanding what He wants to reveal to us. Our "spiritual sensor" must be honed through relationship with Him. That's knowledge, wisdom, understanding—gifts of the Holy Spirit. He's always speaking; we're so often not aware. We miss Him.

I find God speaks to me in the words of:
- Loved Ones
- Friends
- Acquaintances
- Strangers
- Songs
- Scripture

So, God speaks to us through Scripture, and it is important then to practice Scripture reading regularly. Scripture study helps us to know the Lord. Sometimes praying is like trying to talk to a stranger. The study of Scripture turns that "stranger into an acquaintance, then a friend, and finally a loved master." Remember Father Knight's assertion that Scripture allows us to "know the mind of God."

Reading Scripture as part of our prayer life can cause the words of the Bible to take on life, and that allows us to experience oneness with our Creator.

Offer your day to God each morning: "Lord, I dedicate my day to You, as I dedicate my life to You. Do with me what You will." Then everything you do is a prayer!

In His Love

GROWING UP, I learned a healthy respect for the United States Military because of my dad and my brother. My dad had been drafted during the Korean conflict, though he never deployed. I remember my mom using his old "o.d. green" Army laundry bag for our laundry when I was very young. He used to love old war movies, and my brother and I would watch them with him. He didn't really say much about respecting the Services and Service Members, but we could sense it. My brother and I played "Army" all the time as kids. He always outranked me. We were always in World War II. We were always the Americans: saving ourselves, our platoon, our battalion, our country. We spent many hours in make-believe battles, and we always won 'cause we were the good guys!

Through my active-duty Army husband, I've learned up close what it means to be a good guy. In the military, laying down one's life for a friend is not just a platitude; it's a real possibility. The sacrifices required of a military life are big ones, even in time of peace. But in time of war, in the heat of battle, lives are often lost—and some are saved, due to the extraordinary bravery and selflessness of others.

It's been said that a soldier fights in battle not for his country, or the flag, or any cause, but for his buddies to his left and right. That's love; and in some cases, it can mean the ultimate sacrifice.

❖

This is meant for women, wives who must endure while their husbands go off to a foreign land in defense of our country. That is where we find ourselves now. I am a veteran of six deployments beginning in 1990 with Operation Desert Shield/Desert Storm. With a three-year-old daughter and an infant son, I was left seemingly alone to cope with life's daily routines, joys, and challenges. And, of course, to deal with the fears for my husband, the rest of the service members and families involved, and our nation.

If you have never gone through this, it sounds overwhelming. It seemed, initially, that way to me. But, through that experience, I learned a lot about letting go and turning things over to God. Through that experience I learned to put myself and my family in His hands in a way I'd never done before. It's the way it should always be. We have no control over what others may do to us through their own willful acts; we don't know when our lives will end. But with our Lord in our lives, what others do to us and our mortal shells doesn't really matter in comparison with eternal realities. We must remember that God wants us Home with Him at the appointed time. What men do need not really concern us if we trust in the Lord.

Give your life to God; trust in His mercy and love. Remember, as I learned during that trying time, you are never alone. I am not going to tell you that you won't be lonely. I have a distinct memory of sitting on the floor in our upstairs hallway with one child in the room at the end of the hall to my right and the other child in the room at the opposite end of the hall. We were all crying. I couldn't take it anymore, I thought. And through my tears and frustration and loneliness and fear, I prayed. And I knew underneath all that pain, God was with me, and He was listening. Now that I think of it, He was probably weeping, too. But I knew He was there. I cannot explain how; it was more than imagination, more than a feeling. It was truth. I believe the Holy Spirit's presence was there. It ministered to my spirit.

That's why I wrote this book—to remind you that God is with you, and you will be ministered to if only you seek Him. Let's seek Him together. Let's look in His Word and find wisdom and comfort and peace.

◆

PRAYER SERVICE FOR OUR TROOPS

I base the following prayer service for our Troops on the Mothers' Prayers service. I borrowed the format and the concept of physically placing loved ones' names in a basket at the foot of the Cross as is done in the Mothers' Prayers paraliturgy. This step is optional, but it is always so moving and meaningful during Mothers' Prayers that I would encourage it for the Troop Prayer Service if the group is small. It's harder to do and more time consuming with a crowd.

The service and meditations follow for your use.

Required items: Bible, Crucifix, words for song(s), lit candle, basket and slips of paper for names if used.

Prayer to the Holy Spirit

Holy Spirit of the Living God,
Give us wisdom to know Your Will.
Give us strength to do Your Will.
Give us the words to defend of our faith and spread the Good News of God's love.
Holy Spirit, increase our knowledge of You and thus our gratitude will increase.
Help us to advance Your kingdom; may we always give glory to Your Name.

Fill us with the peace that passes all understanding, so there is no room for fear, no place for anxiety or apprehension.

We place all our trust in You. In Jesus's precious and Holy Name, we pray. Amen.

❖

Prayer for Protection from All Evil

Father of Mercy, Creator of the Universe, Lord of All—deliver us from evil.

Renew our minds so that we can only recall the might of Your holy arm, Your omnipotence, Your infinite love for us.

Whom shall we fear? Of whom should we be afraid?

We place ourselves completely in Your presence.

May we always know of Your concern for us all. We pray for these things in the Name of Jesus, Your Son. Amen.

❖

Prayer for Forgiveness

Lord Jesus,
Forgive us our sins.
Forgive us for the harm we've caused others, ourselves, and You.
We never want to hurt anyone,
Especially not You.
And so we humbly ask Your forgiveness.
We are sorry for our sins.
Your mercy far surpasses Your justice, which is itself perfect.
We are so grateful for Your mercy and Your love. Amen.

❖

Prayer to Be of One Heart and Mind

Unite us, Lord, in Your love. We gather together for the same purpose.

And so we ask You to wipe away anything that may spoil the unity and focus of our meeting this day.

Unite us in mind, in heart, in love for You and our Brothers and Sisters.
We ask this of You, Lord Jesus. Amen.

◆

We Praise God in Song

(Praise hymn/patriotic song)

◆

We Pray to Be United with People of Faith

Dear Lord, We unite our prayers and intentions with all of the faithful throughout the world who are praying for our soldiers this day and every day. We praise You and thank You for the hope we have because of the faith with which You've blessed us. This faith allows us to bring our soldiers to You, asking what's best for them, asking Your Will for them. Amen.

❖

We Read from Scripture

(See "Psalms for Reflection," beginning on page 123 and "Thoughts & Scripture Meditations" beginning on page 156.)

❖

We Thank God for Our Gifts

Thank You, God of Power and Might.
Thank You for the gift of freedom, for the privilege of being an American, for the right to gather and pray as a group of Believers in You. What marvelous gifts! May we never take them for granted. And may we never take for granted those soldiers who so selflessly serve our country and defend others who could not defend themselves. Amen.

❖

Chapter 10 | In His Love

We Place Our Loved Ones in God's Hands

Lord, Jesus, We come before you as concerned citizens and Christians, as ones who love our soldiers. We thank You for them—they are precious gifts to us, our country, and the world.

Help us, Lord, always to remember this, especially now while we are at war. Help them to be strong, Lord.

And help us all—those deployed and those at home—to know that You are always with us—sharing in the joys and the sorrow; joining us in the laughter and weeping with us in the pain.

Please give those of us gathered here today "all the graces we need to fulfill Your plans for our lives and for our duties within our families. You are Almighty God." You can do anything.

"So we turn to You in faith and love knowing that You will answer our prayers. Lord, let us always remember how much You love us and our soldiers,

and how You urge us to come to You" with our cares and concerns.

"Come to Me," You say, "All you who labor and are burdened and I will give you rest."

◈

Petitions

Submit either general intentions aloud or place names/petitions in the basket.

Pray for the safety of those deployed, healing of the wounded, repose of the souls of the departed, grace and protection for all the above groups' families and loved ones, peace in our world and our nation, the victims of war, the soldiers who stay back to support us, and for their families.

If petitions are placed in the basket, it should be placed at the foot of the Cross at this time.

◈

Psalms for Reflection

Psalm 3:9 *Salvation is from the Lord! May your blessing be upon your people! Selah*

Upon Your people bestow Your blessings! He's already saved us through His Son. We are a blessed people. You and yours are blessed!

❖

Psalm 4:9 *In peace I will lie down and fall asleep for you alone, Lord, make me secure.*

Pray this when you're having trouble sleeping while your husband's gone. Lie down, get under your cozy covers—and recite this verse of the psalm. Say it out loud. Then affirm it with an "Amen"!

❖

Psalm 5:12–13 *Then all who trust in you will be glad and forever shout for joy. You will protect them and those will rejoice in you who love your name.*

For you, Lord, bless the just one; you surround him with favor like a shield.

Teach this to your children—recite it every day. Talk to your kids about what a great guy their dad is—it'll make you all feel better. Thank God for the wonderful man you married!

❖

Psalm 6:4–5 *My soul too is shuddering greatly—and you, Lord, how long...? Turn back, Lord, rescue my soul; save me because of your mercy.*

"How long will it be before You answer my prayer?" Even the psalmist asks this of our Lord. This reminds us that we don't know everything. We're not in charge! How could we ever presume we are in control? We must give ourselves over to our God. In His hands is the safest place to be. Find comfort there. But, you always get to ask Him, "How long?" remembering that God's timing is perfect.

❖

Psalm 7:18 *I will thank the Lord in accordance with his justice; I will sing the name of the Lord Most High.*

Be thankful for your life and your knowledge and awareness of your dependence on God.

❖

Psalm 8:2 *O Lord, our Lord, how awesome is your name through all the earth! I will sing of your majesty above the heavens with the mouths of babes and infants.*

Praising the Lord is an important part of prayer that is often neglected. We pray for things and people, and hopefully, we offer prayers of thanksgiving. Don't forget to praise the Creator of all; He who loves you—YOU—so much; His only Son died for you. Yes, as the saying goes, God loves you as if you were His one and *only*. He knows you better than anyone ever could because He knows your heart. Scary thought? Not if you realize He loves you anyway! There's nothing you can do to stop Him from loving you. He can be angry, disappointed, saddened by a thought or an action, but He'll never stop loving you. Praise the Lord! Amen.

Psalm 9:8–11 *The Lord rules forever, has set up his throne for judgment. It is he who judges the world with justice, who judges the peoples with fairness. The Lord is the stronghold for the oppressed, a stronghold in times of trouble. Those who know your name trust in you; you never forsake those who seek you, Lord.*

Take comfort that the Lord is involved in all our lives. Take comfort knowing that He'll never forsake us. Talk to Him when you're troubled. Talk to Him about everything, every day. You can't get to know someone if you don't talk to each other. That's prayer. Pray for a deeper knowledge of God.

Psalm 11:7 *The Lord is just and loves just deeds; the upright will see his face.*

Seeing God's face is something we should all be planning on if we believe His promises. We are not at Home on this earth. We are on a journey. Walk with the Lord, humbly and completely. Sometimes you've got to pick up your cross to walk with Him. But, as a friend once told me, often Jesus picks up the other end of that cross.

◆

Psalm 12:7–8 *The promises of the Lord are sure, silver refined in a crucible, silver purified seven times. You, O Lord, protect us always; preserve us from this generation.*

Anyone in a position of power who thinks they have control over another's destiny is sadly deluded. Give your life to our Lord, and you begin to see how futile it is to grasp at or clutch power. Earthly power means nothing in the context of eternity and where we'll spend it! And who has true dominion over all?

◆

Psalm 13:2–3, 6 *How long, Lord? Will you utterly forget me? How long will you hide your face from me? How long must I carry sorrow in my soul, grief in my heart day after day? How long will my enemy triumph over me? But I trust in your mercy. Grant my heart joy in your salvation, I will sing to the Lord, for he has dealt bountifully with me!*

We're only human. God knows our frailties, our limitations. It is not a sin to ask "when?" or "how long?" must I or someone I love endure suffering? No, but we must trust that the Lord is with us in those times. He can send angels to minister to us and those we love. Seek the Lord always. He does not fail.

◆

Psalm 16:2, 8–9 *I say to the Lord, you are my Lord, you are my only good. I* *keep the Lord always before me; with him at my right hand, I shall never be shaken. Therefore my heart is glad, my soul rejoices; my body also dwells secure.*

A prayer of confidence. Not in ourselves but in the power of the Lord. He'll be our strength if we ask Him.

❖

Psalm 17:6–9 *I call upon you; answer me, O God. Turn your ear to me; hear my speech. Show your wonderful mercy, you who deliver with your right arm those who seek refuge from their foes. Keep me as the apple of your eye; hide me in the shadow of your wings from the wicked who despoil me. My ravenous enemies press upon me;*

Of course, you will ask the Lord for protection—for yourself and those you love. What a marvelous prayer to contemplate. He'll be there for whatever you truly need. Believe.

❖

Psalm 19:8–11 *The law of the Lord is perfect, refreshing the soul. The decree of the Lord is trustworthy, giving wisdom to the simple. The precepts of the Lord are right, rejoicing the heart. The command of the Lord is clear, enlightening the eye. The fear of the Lord is pure, enduring forever. The statues of the Lord are true, all of them just; More desirable than gold, than a hoard of purest gold, Sweeter also than honey or drippings from the comb.*

Words to hold in your heart. To remember no matter what's going on in your life. And where will you find the law, the decree, the precepts, the command of the Lord? And where will you learn fear of the Lord and that all His ordinances are true? In His Word. Read your Bible every day.

❖

Psalm 20:8–9 *Some rely on chariots, others on horses, but we on the name of*

Chapter 10 | In His Love

the Lord our God. They collapse and fall, but we stand strong and firm.

Strong in the name of the Lord. Trusting in Him is better than any earthly thing. Period.

◆

Psalm 22:28–32 *All the ends of the earth will remember and turn to the Lord; All families of nations will bow low before him. For kingship belongs to the Lord, the ruler of the nations. All who sleep in the earth will bow low before God; All who have gone down into the dust will kneel in homage. And I will live for the Lord; my descendants will serve you. The generation to come will be told of the Lord, that they may proclaim to a people yet unborn the deliverance you have brought.*

You'd never guess this is the end of the psalm that begins, "My God, my God, why have you forsaken me?" We all go through tough times of fear and doubt. Jesus did in the Garden at Gethsemane. And that should give us hope. The low moments where you're not feeling so strong or so sure? Those are natural, part of being human. Everyone has those moments. Everyone. Even Jesus.

❖

Psalm 23 *A psalm of David. The Lord is my shepherd; there is nothing I lack. In green pastures he makes me lie down; to still waters he leads me; he restores my soul. He guides me along right paths for the sake of his name. Even though I walk through the valley of the shadow of death, I will fear no evil, for you are with me; your rod and your staff comfort me. You set a table before me in front of my enemies; You anoint my head with oil; my cup overflows. Indeed, goodness and mercy will pursue me all the days of my life; I will dwell in the house of the Lord for endless days.*

❖

Psalm 24:10 *Who is the king of glory? The Lord of hosts, he is the king of glory. Selah*

The whole psalm is awesome. I like the final question and the (to some) obvious answer. I guess it's our job to make that obvious to everyone. Start with your kids. Read the Word to them. Discuss your faith with them. Pray with them and for them, and for their dad.

Psalm 25:4–6 *Make known to me your ways, Lord; teach me your paths. Guide me by your fidelity and teach me, for you are God my savior, for you I wait all the day long. Remember your compassion and your mercy, O Lord, for they are ages old.*

This is one for the Holy Spirit. We want to know God as best as is humanly possible. So, Holy Spirit, teach us and guide us as to what You would have us do and what You would have us say. This is a prayer for wisdom and discernment—gifts of the Holy

Spirit. The Lord is just waiting for us to ask for His spiritual gifts. He wants to heap them on us. You will find new strength in the Lord if you just ask for it!

❖

Psalm 28:6–7 *Blessed be the Lord, who has heard the sound of my pleading. The Lord is my strength and my shield, in whom my heart trusts. I am helped, so my heart rejoices; with my song I praise him.*

Speaking of trust...you will find help from Him, if you ask. And it will be the help you need, not the help you think you need. But you have to trust.

❖

Psalm 29: 1–2, 11 *A psalm of David. Give to the Lord, you sons of God, give to the Lord glory and might; Give to the Lord the glory due his name. Bow down before the Lord's splendor! May the Lord give might to his people; may the Lord bless his people with peace!*

Just a beautiful psalm of praise. I like the idea of God's voice breaking mighty trees like twigs or toothpicks. That gives me a concrete concept to wrap my tiny, mortal mind around when considering God's power. It is insufficient, but it helps give a general idea.

❖

Psalm 30:2, 13 *I praise you, Lord, for you raised me up and did not let my enemies rejoice over me. So that my glory may praise you and not be silent. O Lord, my God, forever will I give you thanks.*

He heals us. Maybe physically, maybe not. But spiritually, if you ask it of Him, He always heals. In that healing, God is glorified. Sometimes that's why we're in need of healing—so the glory of God can be revealed—to us and to those witnessing our transformation!

❖

Psalm 31:24a *Love the Lord, all you who are faithful to him.*

It's not an order. It's a plea! The psalmist pleads with us to love the Lord as He longs to be loved. He longs for us to know Him. Great will be our reward.

◆

Psalm 32:1–2 *Of David. A maskil. Blessed is the one whose fault is removed, whose sin is forgiven. Blessed be the man to whom the Lord imputes no guilt, in whose spirit is no deceit.*

What relief to know your sins are forgiven! That God forgives and truly forgets is such a thought to be treasured. It's like you never sinned when you're truly sorry. And you get to start fresh! What a blessing, a gift. What a God we serve.

◆

Psalm 33:1–12, 22 *Rejoice, you righteous, in the Lord; praise from the upright is fitting. Give thanks to the*

Chapter 10 | In His Love

Lord on the harp; on the ten-stringed lyre offer praise. Sing to him a new song; skillfully play with joyful chant. For the Lord's word is upright; all his works are trustworthy. He loves justice and right. The earth is full of the mercy of the Lord. By the Lord's word the heavens were made; by the breath of his mouth all their host. He gathered the waters of the sea as a mound; he sets the deep into storage vaults. Let all the earth fear the Lord; let all who dwell in the world show him reverence. For he spoke, and it came to be, commanded, and it stood in place. The Lord foils the plan of nations, frustrates the designs of peoples. But the plan of the Lord stands forever, the designs of his heart through all generations. Blessed is the nation whose God is the Lord, the people chosen as his inheritance. May your mercy, Lord, be upon us; as we put our hope in You.

The United States of America was founded by men who believed in God, men who believed the formation of this independent nation was blessed by God. We believe that, too, don't we?

❖

Psalm 35:1–6 *Of David. Oppose, O Lord, those who oppose me; war upon those who make war upon me. Take up the shield and buckler; rise up in my defense. Brandish lance and battle-ax against my pursuers. Ay to my soul, "I am your salvation." Let those who seek my life be put to shame and disgrace. Let those who plot evil against me be turned back and confounded. Make them like chaff before the wind, with the angel of the Lord driving them on. Make their way slippery and dark, with the angel of the Lord pursuing them.*

A prayer to share with your husband. As the battle is imminent, the man of the house will find comfort in these words.

❖

Psalm 37:23–24 *The valiant one whose steps are guided by the Lord, who will* *delight in his way, may stumble, but he will never fall, for the Lord of hosts holds his hand.*

May the hand of the Lord sustain our Soldiers, Sailors, Airmen, and Marines; and may we be sustained, as well, by the Lord's hand. Amen.

❖

Psalm 37:39-40 *The salvation of the righteous is from the Lord, their refuge in a time of distress. The Lord helps and rescues them, rescues and saves them from the wicked, because they take refuge in him.*

Take refuge in the Lord, you who are weary! Crying babies, troubled teenagers, broken down cars, plumbing problems, sadness, loneliness—give it all to God. And while you are presenting these things to Him, take refuge there. He's bigger than any problem, certainly stronger than you. Give it to Him and take refuge from the storm. And give your Soldier to Him.

Psalm 40:2–4 *Surely, I wait for the Lord; who bends down to me and hears my cry, Draws me up from the pit of destruction, out of the muddy clay, Sets my feet upon rock, steadies my steps, and puts a new song in my mouth, a hymn to our God. Many shall look on in fear and they shall trust in the Lord.*

"Many shall look on in awe and trust in the Lord" because of you! Because you turn to the Lord, and He in all His goodness and holiness, so far beyond us, stoops to hear your cries. Incredible, but true. And He shall be glorified by this. Others may come to know and to turn to God through your faith in Him. All we want to do is glorify Your name, O Lord. In our helplessness, You are our strength. Alleluia!

Psalm 41:14 *Blessed be the Lord, the God of Israel, from all eternity and forever. Amen. Amen.*

A hymn of praise we should recite throughout life.

◆

Psalm 42:6 *Why are you downcast, my soul; why do you groan within me? Wait for God, for I shall again praise him, my savior and God.*

Sometimes we need to give ourselves a 'good talking to'. Allow yourself moments to cry and lament, but then remember Who is in control and give your life back to Him.

◆

Psalm 44:5–9 *You are my king and my God, who bestows victories on Jacob. Through you we batter our foes; through your name we trample our adversaries. Not in my bow do I trust, nor does my sword bring me victory. You have brought us victory over our enemies, shamed those who hate us. In God we have boasted all the daylong; your name we will praise forever. Selah*

Some encouragement for your Soldier. And for you.

❖

Psalm 46: 2–4 *God is our refuge and our strength, an ever-present help in distress. Thus we do not fear, though earth be shaken and mountains quake to the depths of the sea, though its waters rage and foam and mountains totter at its surging. Selah*

You can't look with earthly eyes at what's going on around you and not be frightened. So, don't look with earthly eyes. See with spiritual eyes that which is the glory, the goodness, the greatness of the Lord! And then, we need not fear. Always there, strengthening us with His love, filling us with His peace, He is waiting to be your refuge. Run!

❖

Psalm 47:8–10 *For God is king over all the earth; sing hymns of praise. God rules over the nations; God sits upon* his holy throne. The princes of the peoples assemble with the people of the God of Abraham. For the shields of the earth belong to God, highly exalted.

Mere mortals who, thinking they are in control of their destinies or their nations' destinies, are sadly deluded. We must remember that the wise leader seeks God's counsel, and the great leader knows his own limitations but also his responsibilities. And, without God, he shouldn't even bother to get up in the morning.

❖

Psalm 56:5, 10–12 *I praise the word of God; I trust in God, I do not fear. What can mere flesh do to me? My foes turn back when I call on you. This I know: God is on my side. I praise the word of God, I praise the word of the Lord. In God I trust, I do not fear. What can man do to me?*

Of course, we must have reverence for human life. There is a divine spark in each of us. God loves each of us as if we are the

Drowning in Lemonade

only one He's created. But, we must not fear the end of our earthly existence. This is not our Home. We are headed at an unknown time to eternity with the Father. And that's when all our suffering, pain, frustration will be wiped away. No matter what we endure here that hurts us, it will all seem like a distant dream—or that it happened in the blink of an eye—when we're in heaven! What can flesh do against me or those I love? Because it's not about the flesh, it's about the spirit. And the Lord longs to have us join Him in His eternal Home where nothing can harm us—ever.

❖

Psalm 57:8–12 *My heart is steadfast, God, my heart is steadfast. I will sing and chant praise. Awake, my soul; awake, lyre and harp! I will wake the dawn. I will praise you among the peoples, Lord; I will chant your praise among the nations. For your mercy towers to the heavens; your faithfulness reaches to the skies. Exalt yourself over*

Chapter 10 | In His Love

the heavens, God; may your glory appear above all the earth.

Another hymn of praise. Remember to praise Him every day. If we were to praise God all day, every day, it could not be enough. He created you; He loves you! Awesome!

❖

Psalm 59:10, 17–18 *My strength, for you I watch; you, God, are my fortress, my loving God...But I shall sing of your strength, extol your mercy at dawn, For you are my fortress, my refuge in time of trouble. My strength, your praise I will sing; you, God, are my fortress, my loving God.*

Remember that He is with you always! Whenever you need Him, He's already there. There may be instances in your life where God will not just give you strength; He will be your strength when you have none left of your own. Call upon the name of the Lord.

You may have many moments of distress. Seek your stronghold—and don't despair!

❖

Psalm 62: 2–4 *Shout joyfully to God, all the earth; sing of his glorious name; give him glorious praise. Say to God: "How awesome your deeds! Before your great strength your enemies cringe. All the earth falls in worship before you; they sing of you, sing of your name!" Selah*

Trust—it's so scary, isn't it? Take that leap of faith, you think, but what if no one catches you after you leave the precipice? But He will! There is nothing to fear with God as the One you depend on. Anything you ask, for your spiritual good, will be given to you. Pray for the gift of trusting in the Lord's faithfulness and love. You won't be disappointed.

❖

Chapter 10 | In His Love

Psalm 63:2–4 *O God, you are my God— it is you I seek! For you my body yearns; for you my soul thirsts, In a land parched, lifeless, and without water. I look to you in the sanctuary to see your power and glory. For your love is better than life; my lips shall ever praise you!*

Use some of this time alone to get closer to your Lord. That's what these alone times are often for—how generous! Giving us time to realize how much we need Him. Some people never learn. But you have been given time to learn, or remember, how much we need God in our lives.

❖

Psalm 66:2–4 *Shout joyfully to God, all the earth; sing of his glorious name; give him glorious praise. Say to God: "How awesome your deeds! Before your great strength your enemies cringe. All the earth falls in worship before you; they sing of you, sing of your name!" Selah*

Your enemies pay an unwilling tribute of praise. Isn't that wonderful?

❖

Psalm 67:2 *May God be gracious to us and bless us; may his face shine upon us. Selah*

Forgive us our sins, Lord. Forgive us for not coming to You sooner. For our pride in thinking we were in charge—have mercy on us. And never turn away, Lord, for we now realize how very much we need You. You sustain us, Lord. Alleluia!

❖

Psalm 68:33–36 *You kingdoms of earth, sing to God; chant the praises of the Lord, Selah Who rides the heights of the ancient heavens, Who sends forth his voice as a mighty voice? Confess the power of God, whose majesty protects Israel, whose power is in the sky. Awesome is God in his holy place, the God of Israel, who gives power and strength to his people. Blessed be God!*

Read it and believe!

◆

Psalm 72:18–19 *Blessed be the Lord God, the God of Israel, who alone does wonderful deeds. Blessed be his glorious name forever; may he fill all the earth with his glory. Amen and amen.*

Amen!

◆

Psalm 77:2–3, 12–14 *I cry aloud to God, I cry to God to hear me. On the day of my distress I seek the Lord. I will recall the deeds of the Lord; yes, recall your wonders of old. I will ponder all your works; on your exploits I will meditate. Your way, God, is holy; what god is as great as our God?*

Ever feel that way (vss. 2–11)? Like you've been abandoned? Like no one is as sad and lonely as you are right now? Especially as you find yourself in the middle of the night. Go ahead, cry to God, whine, complain, lament. He can take it. And, it's good for you. But, when the long night is over, remember the verses (14–21) following. Our God is an awesome God—nothing can defeat Him or our spirit when connected to His!

❖

Psalm 84:12–13 *For a sun and shield is the Lord God, bestowing all grace and glory. The Lord withholds no good thing from those who walk without reproach. O Lord of hosts, blessed the man who trusts in you!*

Happy? Do you ever really feel happy? Your beloved is gone, for who knows how long, and in danger from all sorts of snares and weapons. You worry, you're lonely. Happy?! Yes, for happy—joyful—are those who trust in the Lord God Almighty.

❖

Psalm 86:3–7 *Be gracious to me, Lord; to you I call all the day. Gladden the* soul of your servant; to you, Lord, I lift up my soul. Lord, you are good and forgiving, most merciful to all who call on you. Lord, hear my prayer; listen to my cry for help. On the day of my distress I call to you, for you will answer me.*

Lift up your soul to the Creator of all. Offer it up to Him, along with your husband, and kids, and worries, and troubles. God wants us to give it all to Him. He wants to interject Himself in your life. He's waiting to be asked by each of us. He's crazy about you! Your burdens really do become light when God is the One on Whom you lean.

❖

Psalm 86:15–16 *But you, Lord, are a compassionate and gracious God, slow to anger, abounding in mercy and truth. Turn to me, be gracious to me; give your strength to your servant; save the son of your handmaid.*

'Nuff said.

❖

Psalm 89:53 *Blessed be the Lord forever! Amen and amen!*

Amen and amen!

❖

Psalm 91: 1–4 *You who dwell in the shelter of the Most High, who abide in the shade of the Almighty, Say to the Lord, "My refuge and fortress, my God in whom I trust." He will rescue you from the fowler's snare, from the destroying plague, He will shelter you with his pinions, and under his wings you may take refuge; his faithfulness is a protecting shield.*

Ideally, your spouse should have a Bible with him while deployed. If he didn't take one with him, send him one. And highlight this psalm. It is comforting, especially for a warrior.

❖

Chapter 10 | In His Love

Psalm 95:1-7a *Come, let us sing joyfully to the Lord; cry out to the rock of our salvation. Let us come before him with a song of praise, joyfully sing out our psalms. For the Lord is the great God, the great king over all gods, whose hand holds the depths of the heart; who owns the tops of the mountains. The sea and dry land belong to God, who made them, formed them by hand. Enter, let us bow down in worship; let us kneel before the Lord who made us. For he is our God, we are the people he shepherds, the sheep in his hands.*

It is good to be reminded from time to time all that the Lord does for us and has provided for us out of His love for us.

❖

Psalm 96:1-3 *Sing to the Lord a new song; sing to the Lord, all the earth. Sing to the Lord, bless his name; proclaim his salvation day after day. Tell his glory among the nations; among all peoples, his marvelous deeds.*

Yes, it's true, we should all rejoice. Even with all the seeming uncertainty in our lives, we must rejoice. Look at all the blessings in our world and life!

As you get closer to God, things of this world seem less and less important. Your perspective changes and so do your priorities. It is a marvelous process.

And, if you're genuinely changing as you move toward the Lord—growing in knowledge and wisdom—you'll find you don't mind the changes in your behavior or in your values or your language. If God is in you, the change won't be scary. There is peace in such a change. And, as the Disney song says, you can "look at your life through heaven's eyes." The view will be thrilling!

Enjoy the journey to a closer walk with Jesus. That's what this time is about.

Thoughts & Scripture Meditations

Mark 1:9-11

I knew a woman who stopped attending RCIA prior to the Rite of Acceptance. "I can't believe in the Trinity," she said. "It just doesn't make sense to me." I was speechless at first. I never expected this to be her reason. The Trinity is a key precept of our Christian faith. I don't even remember how I defended the Trinity, or if I really could, to someone so adamantly opposed, as I discovered she was in the course of our conversation. Her husband was Catholic; she was raising her children in the faith, but could not believe.

Jesus said, "I am in the Father and the Father is in Me." And Jesus also said that He would send the Holy Spirit. Let us pray for our brothers and sisters who struggle to believe, that they receive the faith, understanding, and wisdom they need in the name of the Father, the Son, and the Holy Spirit. Amen.

Lord, help my unbelief!

❖

1 Samuel 1:6

None of us would intentionally torment and ridicule another human being. But sometimes, without thinking, that is what happens. And we can truly hurt someone else through our actions or words. We can damage their spirit, a part of them we can't see, which is even more fragile than the physical. Best advice when someone has gotten you so angry or frustrated that you can't think straight: keep your mouth closed to avoid "inserting your foot"! And while you're at it, pray silently for the "peace that passes all understanding" to get you through this situation without harming another individual. We can kill the enthusiasm and self-worth in a person as surely as we can take a life. Instead, we

Chapter 11 | Thoughts & Scripture Meditations

want to be pro-life. We are called to be life-giving examples of Christ's love to others, no matter how indignant we become. Yet, even when we think we have a right to be, not speaking bitter words aloud but silently speaking words of supplication to the Lord is our best reaction to anger.

Holy Spirit, teach me what to say.

❖

Pro-Life Prayer

May the Creator of the Universe,
The God of all that is good,
The Lord of all creation,
The Victor, the Savior,
The Lamb of God,
The Alpha and the Omega,
The Great Physician,
The Perfect Healer,
The Good Shepherd, Our Father,
Our Brother, Our Friend,
Our Defender, Our Advocate,
Our Light, Our Way,

Our Truth, Our Life
Bless and protect His little ones.
May He surround them with angels,
Whether in heaven in His presence,
Or on earth in their mother's womb.

May we never lose hope in and always work for the day when our nation humbly turns to defend the unborn.

We ask this in Jesus's Holy Name. Amen.

~ L. MacFarland, 2005

1 Samuel 1:19-20

Unanswered prayers—why do so many people wonder why God "never" answers their prayers? There are many reasons. One is that, when the answer is no, we don't want to accept it. Another is that we pray for the wrong things! God knows what we need much more than we do. Praying that His Will be done and that we accept His

Chapter 11 | Thoughts & Scripture Meditations

Will is the best prayer. It's also the biggest leap of faith. For it is a test of our faith.

God wants us to rely on Him. We need to place ourselves and our loved ones in His care. And then, stop worrying. Stop pretending we know what's best for us. Stop trying to tell God what we think is the best solution. Pray for wisdom and acceptance. Pray for God's peace within you and pray for patience. These are the things that will not be denied when we earnestly seek them in His Name.

Father, may You be glorified when we pray in Jesus's Name.

1 Samuel 3:8

We've been told that parents are a child's first and best teachers. It is so very important to share our faith, knowledge, values, and beliefs with them.

Children are entrusted to us for such a short time. And we don't get to say, "It's too hard; I'm not going to raise them," or, "It's too much trouble, let them fend for themselves." As loving, responsible Christian parents, we have the wondrous burden of giving them the best of ourselves. Spending time in prayer before we speak, before we start our day with them, asking for the Lord's assistance, the Holy Spirit's gifts, is best thing we can do for our kids. We need to educate ourselves, too. Faith formation classes should be ongoing. There is always something to learn about our faith, the Bible, ourselves. If we don't feel comfortable answering our children's questions, we may not encourage them to ask. Consider a Bible study or theology course through your church.

Lord, give me insight and wisdom, so I might always discern Your holy and true Will. ~ St. Francis of Assisi

Samuel 4:11

God does not punish us for our sins by giving us fatal diseases or unhappy lives. Indeed, these are the consequences for our

Chapter 11 | Thoughts & Scripture Meditations

sin or the sins of mankind and are the things He tries to protect us from with His Law. If we really contemplate the state of our world, we can witness the love our Lord has for us in the ways He tries to protect us from the "wages" of sin. As Eli warned his sons, sin will destroy us. A sin never affects just us. There are always others adversely affected by actions counter to God's Law. God does not want for us to encounter loss, nor does He want us to destroy that which He has created. The sin of an individual, the sins of mankind do both. Let us return to the Lord, penitent and contrite, wanting to live in the world as our loving God intended.

Lord, show me the Way!

❖

1 Samuel 8:17

We must always think morally. We must think about what's best for us, for those we care about, and for our world. Choosing to be a Christian, choosing to love our brothers and sisters—these choices must be deliberate. The excuse, "I didn't know" may ring a little hollow once devastation passes.

Defending the less able, the afflicted, the young is a necessary part of our lives in God's world. You may not be a leader, but you don't have to follow in ways that run counter to your values and beliefs. This is what the Lord requires of us: "to do justice, love mercy, walk humbly with God" (Micah 6:8). These three things will necessarily include responsibility for our fellow man.

Be my strength, O Lord, so I may do Your Will.

❖

1 Samuel 9:17, 10:1

Not too many leaders are chosen today as Saul was chosen by God. A prophet anoints him with oil telling him that God says he will rule and protect God's people. We can all pray for wisdom, and certainly if we are in positions of authority, we'd better! Whether it is as a supervisor or manager, a coach of young people, or a parent, wisdom

Chapter 11 | Thoughts & Scripture Meditations

while we're in charge is the best thing to pray for!

It should be a humbling moment when we are put in charge of someone else's welfare. With God's help, with the Holy Spirit's gifts, with Jesus's gentle example, we can be leaders and role models in the lives of others. They should see Jesus in us; we ought to be living examples of dependence on the Lord for our actions and decision making, for our very lives. That's the kind of leader, the sort of Christian, to which we can all aspire.

Dear Jesus, may I always be inspired by Your gentle example.

About the Author

LYNDA MACFARLAND is an Army wife of 28 years and counting. This includes four nonconsecutive tours, for a total of 14 years, in Germany at various locations, much to her family's delight!

Lynda and her husband, Sean, are the proud parents of Maggie, who is married to an Infantry Officer, and Philip, who recently graduated from the US Military Academy. Maggie, her husband, and Philip are doing very well, and Lynda and her husband are quite proud of these young adults.

Lynda's interests include reading, writing, and singing, as well as working to improve the quality of life for our awesome Army families by means of her role as a 'professional volunteer'.

Her proudest achievements thus far include implementing programs to support

About the Author

her husband's brigade combat team families during its 2006–2007 deployment to Iraq and writing an article that was published in *The Word Among Us* magazine. The article addresses the role her faith plays in meeting the challenges of living an Army life.

Lynda is currently living in Arlington, Virginia while Sean is deployed to Afghanistan.

Resources

IF YOU NEED HELP

If you or someone you love suffers with depression and is in need of immediate confidential help, call:

Veterans Crisis Line: 1.800.273.8225, then press 1
    Website:
    www.veteranscrisisline.net/ChatTermsOf Service.aspx

Military OneSource: 1.800.342.9647
    Website:
    www.militaryonesource.mil

Additional resources can be located at: www.frontlinefaithproject.org

Made in United States
Orlando, FL
06 September 2023